In the age of information, ignorance is a choice -

Donny Miller

By Ellie Grey

© Ellie Grey

We are constantly reassured by doctors, health professionals and mainstream media that nearly everything they recommend is "safe and effective." But is this truly the case?

In an age where information is readily available from countless sources, why is it so difficult to uncover the full truth? Why is it challenging to find comprehensive studies, detailed ingredient lists, and information on the potential negative side effects of vaccines? Why can't we easily access knowledge about mammograms, smear tests, sunscreens, biopsies, and medications? The reason is simple: this information is often hidden from us.

I have created this book not to discourage anyone from conducting their own research but to make this information more accessible. Search engines frequently censor negative links or websites related to alternative practices and lifestyles to protect their sponsors - the pharmaceutical companies.

Consider this: The average general practitioner who has completed medical school spends only about 15 hours learning about vaccines and this education is often derived from biased pharmaceutical sources. Relying entirely on a doctor or nurse who might struggle to list three ingredients in a vaccine is not how we should approach our health. We need to take the initiative to research and uncover the truth behind the numerous misleading claims.

When cancer charities conduct research on smear tests or sunscreen companies test the safety of their own ingredients, we do not receive unbiased information.

We are facing an unprecedented crisis. Children are suffering due to their parents' lack of knowledge. For the first time in history, children are not outliving their parents by the average age of death. There has been a dramatic increase in autism, developmental delays, learning disabilities, allergies, asthma, autoimmune diseases, childhood cancers and other chronic, debilitating conditions.

Maybe, we should also look at the correlations between the amount of medications children (and adults) are on. According to Health Survey for England, 48% of adults in the UK has taken at least one prescription drug in the last week and 24% has taken 3 or more prescribed medications in the last week.

Almost 75,000 children in the UK aged between 6-17 are on medications for ADHD. 27,757 children between ages 5-17 were on anti depressants and 12% of UK primary school children aged between 5-11 are on some kind of prescription medications.

More than ever, we are losing a significant portion of the next generation to neurological, neuro-developmental, behavioural and learning disabilities. According to the CDC in 2023, one in six children has one or more developmental disabilities.

Given our access to the most advanced medical treatments in history, what is going wrong? Could it be that the information we can access is severely limited and filtered? Are we being misled, leading to an entire generation of unwell children? Or are we quite simply, being lied to?

Chapter 1 - Introduction
Chapter 2 - Understanding Vaccines
Chapter 3 - Pregnancy
Chapter 4 - Vaccine Ingredients
Chapter 5 - Mammograms
Chapter 6 - Smear Tests
Chapter 7 - Vitamin K
Chapter 8 - Vaccines & Autism
Chapter 9 - Fluoride
Chapter 10 - Breastfeeding & Formula
Chapter 11 - Natural Remedies & Treatments
Chapter 12 - Suncream
Chapter 13 - Microwaves
Chapter 14 - Sunbeds
Chapter 15 - HPV Vaccine
Chapter 16 - Alzheimers Disease & Aluminium
Chapter 17 - ADHD & Vaccines
Chapter 18 - MTHFR Gene

Chapter 1 - Introduction

As a mother of three, my journey has been deeply rooted in curiosity and a relentless pursuit of truth. From the moment I became a parent, I realised the immense responsibility I held in making informed decisions for my children's well-being. This led me to become an avid researcher, committed to uncovering the facts and following true science - unbiased and untainted by conflicting interests.

Living what some might call an alternative lifestyle, I have chosen a path less travelled. I do not vaccinate my children, opting instead for a natural, homeopathic approach to health. Our family life is deeply intertwined with principles of attachment theory and gentle parenting. These choices stem not from a place of rebellion against the mainstream, but from a profound belief in the power of natural remedies and the importance of nurturing our children in an environment of love, understanding, and holistic care.

People often ask why I make these choices. They wonder why I diverge from conventional practices and what fuels my dedication to this path. This book is my answer. It is a comprehensive guide to the decisions I have made and the extensive research that supports them. My intention is not to persuade or convert, but to offer information that is often hidden or dismissed by mainstream channels. I believe that everyone has the right to access this knowledge and make their own informed choices.

In today's world, information is abundant, yet the truth can be elusive. The internet is a vast ocean of data, but finding reliable and unbiased information requires discernment and diligence. Too often, we are presented with "facts" that are heavily influenced by vested interests, particularly in the realms of pharmaceuticals and conventional medicine. This is why I embarked on a mission to sift through the noise and uncover genuine, evidence-based insights.

I am not a medical professional, but I am a passionate seeker of truth. I have spent thousands of hours pouring over studies, scrutinising sources and questioning widely accepted narratives. My goal is to empower others to do the same. To question, to investigate, and to make choices that resonate with their own values and beliefs.

This book covers a range of topics that are central to my family's way of life. From the decision not to vaccinate to our reliance on homeopathic remedies, from the principles of gentle parenting to the skepticism of mainstream medical practices, each chapter delves into the reasoning and research behind these choices. I provide references and resources, encouraging readers to explore further and form their own conclusions.

One of the key issues I address is the often-overlooked biases in scientific research and medical recommendations. Many studies are funded by entities with a financial stake in the outcomes, leading to conclusions that favour their interests. This bias can distort the truth and mislead the public. My aim is to highlight these conflicts of interest and present alternative perspectives that are grounded in genuine science and practical experience.

Moreover, I discuss the rise in chronic health issues among children today - autism, developmental delays, allergies, autoimmune diseases and more. Despite our access to advanced medical treatments, these conditions are becoming increasingly common. I explore potential causes and contributing factors, offering insights that challenge conventional wisdom and suggest new avenues for prevention and treatment.

In sharing my journey, I hope to foster a community of informed and empowered individuals. Whether you share my views or not, I invite you to engage with the content of this book critically and thoughtfully. My purpose is not to provide a definitive guide to parenting, lifestyle or health, but to spark curiosity and encourage a deeper understanding of the choices we make for ourselves and our families. [i]

---

[i] References
- https://www.cdc.gov/ncbddd/developmentaldisabilities/about.html
- https://www.ncbi.nlm.nih.gov/m/pubmed/8679122/ & https://www.ncbi.nlm.nih.gov/m/pubmed/15952931/

Chapter 2 - Understanding Vaccines

"There has never been a single study that proves the antibody response to vaccination is synonymous with immunity."

If there is one thing every parent should know about vaccines, it is this:

There has never been a conclusive study proving that an antibody response from a vaccine equates to true immunity. The entire concept of vaccination rests on this assumption, which falls apart under close examination.

Here's what happens when doctors check your antibody levels (titers) to see if you're immune to a disease: it's more hopeful than scientific. In reality, some studies show that people can still get sick even if they have high levels of antibodies from vaccines. Moreover, babies can't produce a strong antibody response until they're about a year old.

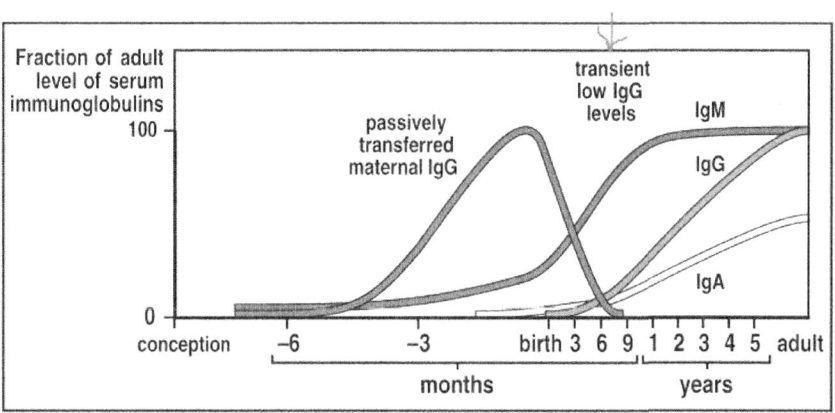

Figure 11-11 Immunobiology, 6/e. (© Garland Science 2005)

The graph above explains this in more detail:
The darker blue line represents the antibodies babies receive from their mothers before birth.

The red line shows that babies start producing their own antibodies (IgM) between 3 and 6 months before birth. However, these are immature and less effective compared to mature antibodies (IgG).

After birth, the baby's own IgG levels start to increase but don't reach significant levels until about one year old.
Maternal antibodies decrease around 3 months, especially if breastfeeding is reduced or stopped. This creates a vulnerable period (highlighted in blue) where infants are more prone to infections, making early vaccines risky.

Antibody response is just one part of the immune system. Vaccines primarily target this response, ignoring the cell-mediated immune system, which is the body's first line of defence against natural infections. Often, the cell-mediated immune system handles infections so effectively that antibodies aren't even needed.

By vaccinating, we repeatedly trigger an unnatural and overstimulating response in the body. This can lead to a pro-allergic, inflammatory state without proven benefits and clear evidence of potential harm.

Focusing too much on the antibody response can confuse the immune system, causing it to function less effectively. This can weaken the cell-mediated immune system, making children more susceptible to infections (especially meningitis) and increasing the risk of autoimmune disorders, where the immune system attacks the body itself.

Understanding Your Immune System: Simplified

TH1 & TH2 Immune Responses

Your immune system has two main types of responses: TH1 and TH2.

- **TH1 Cells**: These help your body fight off viruses and bacteria by attacking the infected cells directly.

- **TH2 Cells**: These help your body fight off parasites and some bacteria by making antibodies.

For your immune system to work well, there needs to be a balance between TH1 and TH2 responses. This balance is called immunostasis, or immune balance.

Vaccines and Immune Balance

Vaccines can disrupt this balance by making TH2 cells more dominant. This can weaken your body's natural defence against infections.

Natural Immunity vs. Vaccine-Induced Immunity

- **Natural Immunity**: When you get infected with something like chickenpox naturally, your body uses a TH1 response to fight it off and remembers how to do it in the future. This gives you permanent immunity and helps create herd immunity, where enough people are immune to stop the disease from spreading.

- **Vaccine-Induced Immunity**: Vaccines often cause a TH2 response. This type of response doesn't create a strong memory in your immune system, which is why they state you need boosters. The vaccine makes your body react quickly (in theory), but it doesn't teach it to remember how to fight the infection in the future.

How T Cells Work

T-cells are a key part of your immune system. They help control and direct how your body fights infections and remembers them. T-helper cells (Th cells) are a type of T cell that coordinates the immune response.

When you get a virus naturally, like measles, your body's TH1 response helps you fight it off with symptoms like fever and rash. This process helps your body learn to fight the virus forever.

However, when you get vaccinated, the vaccine skips the usual way your body fights infections. This causes an emergency TH2 response, which doesn't help your body remember the infection.

Why Not Create Vaccines That Trigger TH1 Response?

The body's natural response to viruses is to externalise and eliminate them. Vaccines don't do this, which is why herd immunity can't be achieved through vaccination alone.

Conclusion

Vaccines can sometimes push infections deeper into the body and make them harder to fight in the long run, potentially leading to chronic illnesses and autoimmune disorders. As Wendy Myers said, "We cannot and will not eradicate all disease with vaccines. We have merely traded acute illnesses from which most recover for chronic illnesses for which modern medicine has no cure."

Simplifying the Effects of Vaccines on the Immune System

How Vaccines Affect Your Immune System

Vaccines can change how your immune system works in a way that might not be healthy. Here's a simple breakdown:

- **Immune System Basics**: Your immune system has two main ways to fight off germs:
    - **TH1 Response**: This is like the front-line soldiers that attack and destroy infected cells.

- - **TH2 Response**: This part makes antibodies that help identify and tag germs for destruction.
- **Vaccination Theory**: When you get vaccinated:
  - The vaccine mostly activates the TH2 response (antibodies).
  - It doesn't activate the TH1 response (the front-line soldiers).

This imbalance can overstimulate the TH2 response, keeping your immune system in a constant state of alert. This can lead to chronic health problems and doesn't provide true immunity.

- **Natural Infection vs. Vaccination**:
  - When a child naturally gets an infection, the TH1 response kicks in first to fight the infection.
  - Then, the TH2 response tags the germs with antibodies, creating lasting immunity without needing boosters.

The TH2 Shift

Vaccines cause a shift in your immune system known as the "TH2 shift," which means:

- Your immune system relies more on antibodies and less on the TH1 response.
- This makes your immune system weaker overall and can make you more susceptible to other infections.

Most people, including many doctors, are not aware of this effect. Scientists know about it but often don't speak out due to fear of damaging their careers.

It is important to remember, if vaccines really gave immunity - you wouldn't need the boosters.

Dr. Russell Blaylock M.D. Neurosurgeon states:

"Bypassing the mucosal aspect of the immune system by directly injecting organisms into the body leads to a corruption in the immune system itself where IgA (Immunoglobulin A) is transmitted into IgE (Immunoglobulin E), and/or the B cells are hyper-activated to produce pathological amounts of self-tracking antibody as well as suppression of cytotoxic T cells 'stealth adapted.' These are formed when vaccine viruses combine with viruses from tissues used to culture them, or when bacteria lose their cell walls when a person takes antibiotics and transform them into 'L forms,' leading to a lack of some critical antigens normally recognised by the cellular immune system."

"Thus, rather than preventing disease, the disease is actually prevented from ever being resolved. Thus, the autoimmune disease you develop is determined by which tissues in the body are attacked by auto-antibodies. If the inside lining of the gastrointestinal tract (the mucosa) is attacked by auto-antibodies, you can develop leaky gut syndrome. Crohn's disease and colitis are also caused by auto-antibody attack of the GI tract itself. If the islet (insulin producing) cells of the pancreas are attacked by auto-antibodies, you develop insulin dependent (juvenile) diabetes."

Chapter 3 - Pregnancy

"It is not known whether the whooping cough vaccine can cause fetal harm when administered to a pregnant woman or can affect reproductive capacity. Tripedia vaccine is NOT indicated for women of child-bearing age."

- Tripedia Vaccine Insert

When your midwife or GP is recommending the Flu Vaccine or the Whooping cough vaccine, do they tell you these facts?

1 - Not a single licensed vaccine has ever been tested on a pregnant woman?

2 - The manufacturers themselves state that they do not recommend vaccines during pregnancy as the damage to the baby is unknown?

3 - The whooping cough vaccine, is not just a single vaccine. It is called Boostrix IPV and it is a 4 in one booster vaccine for Pertussis, Polio, Diptheria and Tetanus ?

4 - The booster vaccine contains - formaldehyde, aluminium hydroxide, sodium chloride, polysorbate 80?

5 - That there is a 4,250% increase in fetal deaths after the flu vaccine?

There are many studies to prove how dangerous it is to receive a vaccine during pregnancy. There is currently no data to suggest that catching the wild strain influenza whilst pregnant can cause a miscarriage or fetal death, but many studies proving that receiving the flu vaccine during pregnancy can.

A study comparison on the two-vaccine 2009/10 influenza season conducted by Dr Neil Z Miller and Paul G King, PhD concluded that thimerosal based vaccines were attributing to the cause of still births and miscarriage in pregnant women.

"Thimerosal has been found to be toxic at very low levels. For example, Parran et al. examined the effects of Thimerosal on cell death in a human neuroblastoma cell line. Following 48 h of a single dose of 4.35 nanomolar Thimerosal (or about 0.87 mcg/kg of mercury) over 50% of cells were dead.

Thus, it is biologically plausible that during the two-vaccine 2009/2010 influenza season, when pregnant women were administered two Thimerosal-containing influenza vaccines each delivering 50 mcg of Thimerosal (or 25 mcg of mercury per dose), the fetus' mercury dose exceeded the EPAs reference dose (0.1 mcg of mercury/kg/day). This overexposure could be a significant contributing factor to some of the reported SABs and SBs. Moreover, the mercury in injected Thimerosal-containing vaccine doses has been found to preferentially bioaccumulate in the fetal tissues. This study demonstrates that depending upon the gestational age, the safety level of mercury (as specified by the EPA's reference dose) may be exceeded by several thousand fold for an early developing fetus during the first trimester to a factor of just over 1 at full-term – even for a single reduced Thimerosal vaccine dose presuming only 50% of the mercury (0.5 mcg) bioaccumulates in the fetus."

Miller goes on to conclude - *"Thus, a synergistic fetal toxicity likely resulted from the administration of both the pandemic (A-H1N1) and seasonal influenza vaccines during the 2009/2010 season."* [ii]

According to the NHS, these are the things you must stay away from in pregnancy -

- High mercury fish, Raw eggs, Unwashed produce, Soft cheese, Paté, Unpasteurised milk, Liver and liver products, X-rays

But apparently, these things are fine -

[ii] - https://www.cdc.gov/vaccines/pubs/pinkbook/downloads/appendices/b/excipient-table-2.pdf)
- http://www.ncbi.nlm.nih.gov/pmc/articles/PMC3888271/
- http://vactruth.com/2012/11/23/flu-shot-spikes-fetal-death/
- http://www.ncbi.nlm.nih.gov/pubmed/23023030
- http://www.ncbi.nlm.nih.gov/pmc/articles/PMC3888271/
- http://het.sagepub.com/content/early/2012/09/12/0960327112455067.abstract
- https://www.ncbi.nlm.nih.gov/pmc/articles/PMC3888271/
https://www.cdc.gov/vaccines/pubs/pinkbook/downloads/appendices/b/excipient-table-2.pdf
11 - http://www.cs.unc.edu/~plaisted/ce/humanity.html
12 - https://www.commonwealthfund.org/publications/issue-briefs/2020/nov/maternal-mortality-maternity-care-us-compared-10-countries

- Formaldehyde, Aluminium hydroxide, Sodium chloride, Polysorbate 80, carcinogens, neurotoxins and toxic ingredients. It doesn't make sense, does it?

The human race is about 300 generations old. At least 290 of those generations had no allopathic pharmaceutical involvement whatsoever, and approximately 298 of those generations, had no vaccines. Yet, the United States has the highest maternal and infant mortality rate in all of the developed countries, the UK is 4th. The lowest of those is Norway, where vaccines are not forcefully pushed upon an expectant parent.

Folic Acid or Folate?

During pregnancy, folic acid is frequently recommended. According to the NHS, "Folic acid is the man-made version of the vitamin folate (also known as vitamin B9). Folate helps the body make healthy red blood cells and is found in certain foods". However, there is a significant difference between natural folate and synthetic folic acid, and it's important to understand these differences.

The Issue with Folic Acid

Folic acid is a synthetic form of vitamin B9, created by the pharmaceutical industry. While it is often added to supplements and fortified foods, it does not work the same way as natural folate. Some research even suggests that individuals with MTHFR (Methylenetetrahydrofolate reductase) gene mutations may struggle to convert folic acid into its active form. This can lead to worsened symptoms and health issues when consuming folic acid.

The Importance of Natural Folate

Natural folate is crucial, especially before and during pregnancy. Obtaining adequate folate three months before conception and during the first trimester can significantly reduce the risk of various health problems in children. Instead of relying on synthetic folic acid, look for supplements containing the bioavailable form of folate known as l-methylfolate. Additionally, include plenty of folate-rich foods in your diet:

- Beans and lentils
- Leafy green vegetables (e.g. raw spinach, cabbage, kale)
- Asparagus
- Romaine lettuce
- Broccoli
- Avocado
- Peas

The Wisdom of Nature

Remember, humans have been reproducing successfully for millennia. Our bodies are not flawed. Decades ago, pregnancies and births occurred without heavy pharmaceutical involvement. It is only in recent times that we have been conditioned to fear pregnancy and birth, benefiting the pharmaceutical industry.

If you maintain a healthy diet, you likely do not need to supplement with synthetic vitamins. It's essential to read the ingredients in your prenatal vitamins, as anything you consume affects your baby.

In conclusion, prioritising natural folate over synthetic folic acid and trusting in the natural processes of your body can support a healthier pregnancy and baby.

Many studies have shown a link between folic acid being taken during pregnancy and a positive MTHFR genetic disposition with the baby when born. (See chapter 18)

Chapter 3 - Vaccine Ingredients

"Administration of aluminium to neonatal mice in vaccine relevant amounts is associated with adverse long term neurological outcomes. A correlation between increasing ASD rates and aluminium (Al) adjuvants in common use in paediatric vaccines in several Western countries. The correlation between ASD rate and Al adjuvant amounts appears to be dose-dependent."

- Journal of Inorganic Biochemistry

---

iii https://www.nhs.uk/medicines/folic-acid/
 - http://www.ncbi.nlm.nih.gov/pubmed/23932735

Unveiling Vaccine Ingredients

Unfortunately, vaccine ingredients include many synthetic chemicals that are known to be toxic to humans, as well as foreign human fragments (from aborted babies) and animal cells and DNA. These ingredients can cause a host of issues, especially when injected.

Intriguingly, the composition of vaccines unveils a complex array of synthetic chemicals, along with foreign human fragments and animal DNA. These components, when injected, can provoke a cascade of health issues.

Within vaccines lie aluminium, mercury, formaldehyde, antibiotics, human fetal cells, GMOs, animal proteins and DNA, glyphosate, Polysorbates, and a plethora of other substances renowned for their carcinogenic and neurotoxic properties.

Unlike food, vaccines are injected directly into muscle tissue, creating a reservoir for slow-release and prolonged antibody stimulation. Remarkably, these ingredients don't merely dissipate; some, like aluminium and mercury, have the propensity to accumulate in the brain over time.

Vaccines contain a variety of synthetic chemicals and biological materials, some of which are known to be toxic. Here is a breakdown of common vaccine ingredients and their potential risks:

Understanding what goes into injections is crucial for making informed decisions about health. Here's a breakdown of some concerning ingredients commonly found in various injections and their potential health risks:

1. Foetal Bovine Serum
This serum is derived from the blood of unborn calves and contains animal DNA. Mixing animal DNA with human DNA could potentially pose a risk of mutation within the body's cells, leading to unpredictable genetic changes.

2. Aluminium
Aluminium is a neurotoxin linked to various health issues, including brain damage, Alzheimer's disease, dementia, seizures, autoimmune disorders, Sudden Infant Death Syndrome (SIDS), and cancer. It accumulates in the brain over time, causing more damage with each exposure.

3. Formaldehyde
Known for its use in embalming and in industrial applications like paint production, formaldehyde is a potent carcinogen. It is also linked to numerous health problems, including gastrointestinal, liver, respiratory, immune, nerve, and reproductive issues. Even small amounts are highly toxic to the human body.

4. Beta-Propiolactone
This chemical is recognised as carcinogenic and is suspected to cause a range of health issues, including problems with the gastrointestinal tract, liver, nervous system, and respiratory system.

5. Antibiotics (Gentamicin Sulfate & Polymyxin B)
While antibiotics are used to treat infections, they can cause allergic reactions that range from mild to life-threatening. These antibiotics, in particular, are known to cause severe allergic responses in some individuals.

6. Genetically Modified Organisms (GMOs)
Some injections contain genetically modified yeast, bacteria, and viral DNA. These GMOs can integrate into human DNA, potentially leading to genetic mutations and allergies.

7. Glutaraldehyde
Glutaraldehyde is a toxic chemical used in various industrial applications, including cold sterilants, disinfectants, and

embalming solutions. It is highly poisonous and has been linked to birth defects in animal studies.

8. Latex Rubber
Latex is known to cause severe allergic reactions in some individuals. Even minimal exposure can trigger significant health responses in those with latex allergies.

9. Peanut & Soybean Oil
These oils are often used as stabilisers in vaccines but are associated with allergies, particularly nut and soy allergies. Exposure can potentially lead to severe allergic reactions.

10. Human and Animal Cells
Some injections contain human fetal cells and animal proteins. The inclusion of these cells is controversial, as it has been suggested they might be linked to conditions like childhood leukemia and diabetes.

11. Mercury (Thimerosal)
Thimerosal, a mercury-based preservative, is extremely toxic even in small doses. It can affect the brain, gut, liver, bone marrow, nervous system, and kidneys. Thimerosal has been linked to various autoimmune and neurological disorders, including autism.

12. Monosodium Glutamate (MSG)
MSG, often found in food, is sometimes used in vaccines as a stabiliser. It is associated with toxic effects, including birth defects, developmental delays, and infertility.

13. Neomycin Sulfate
This antibiotic can cause severe side effects, including permanent hearing loss, nerve damage, and kidney damage. Allergic reactions to neomycin can also be severe, ranging from mild rashes to life-threatening conditions.

14. Phenol/Phenoxyethanol
These chemicals are used as preservatives and in antifreeze. They

are toxic to cells and can damage the immune system, compromising the body's ability to fight off infections.

15. Polysorbate 80, 20, & 60
These emulsifiers are known to cause cancer in animals and have been linked to autoimmune issues and infertility in humans. They can also disrupt the blood-brain barrier, potentially allowing harmful substances to reach the brain.

16. Phenoxyethanol
Commonly used as a preservative, phenoxyethanol is toxic to reproductive organs and can have other adverse health effects.

17. Streptomycin
This antibiotic is used to treat serious bacterial infections but can cause severe side effects, including nerve reactions, vision problems, balance issues, brain damage, and hearing problems.

18. Polymyxin B
Another antibiotic used to treat bacterial infections, Polymyxin B, can lead to nerve damage, hearing loss, and kidney damage.

By understanding these ingredients and their potential risks, we can make more informed decisions about what we choose to put into our and our children's bodies. It's always a good idea to discuss any concerns with a healthcare professional and consider all available information when making health decisions.

Ingestion vs. Injection: Unveiling the Differences

In the realm of pharmaceutical products, understanding precisely what you're administering—especially through injections—is paramount. Vaccines, administered via injection, necessitate a heightened awareness of their constituents. Why? Because research indicates that injected substances are notably more potent than those ingested orally, bypassing the body's natural detoxification pathways.

This injectable nature means a higher retention of vaccine components in the body, circulating through the bloodstream and affecting vital organs and tissues. The resultant acute and chronic inflammation has been implicated in a myriad of modern health ailments, and in severe cases, can even lead to sudden death.

When we consume food, our body possesses a remarkable defence mechanism to eliminate any substances it finds disagreeable. Through actions like urination, coughing, sneezing, sweating, and natural excretion, our system naturally rids itself of unwanted chemicals. However, the story takes a stark turn when substances are injected directly into our bodies. Unlike ingested materials, injected ingredients don't follow the natural detox pathway of our bodies. They evade the mechanisms that would typically flush out toxins. Ingredients like aluminium and mercury, for instance, navigate their way to the brain over time, accumulating and bypassing our body's natural defence mechanisms. In this scenario, our body's innate defences are circumvented, unable to deploy their usual protective measures.

Scientific research underscores that substances injected are significantly more potent than those ingested. Approximately 95% of injected toxins, such as aluminium, swiftly enter the bloodstream from muscle tissue, where they can traverse to vital organs like the brain, heart, kidneys, and liver. Studies indicate that injected aluminium can linger in the body for months, potentially years, inducing chronic health issues by escalating inflammation levels. Contrastingly, when aluminium is ingested through food, water, or air, only around 5% is absorbed into the body, while the majority is efficiently filtered through our body's natural detoxification pathways. This stark difference in absorption rates underscores a crucial distinction between ingestion and injection.

The crux of the matter lies in the fact that injected aluminium cannot be effectively eliminated by the kidneys, unlike its ingested counterpart. Injected aluminium, in the form of nanoparticles, dissolves slowly into an ionic form, making removal challenging, especially when absorbed alongside antigens. In contrast, ingested aluminium, primarily in ionic form, can be swiftly removed by the kidneys. This disparity in removal mechanisms highlights the enduring implications of injection-related toxicity on our health.

Chapter 5 - Mammograms

"Mammography screening has been promoted to the public with a simple promise that it saves lives and breasts by catching the cancers early. There is so much over-diagnosis that the best thing a women can do to lower her risk of becoming a breast cancer patient is to avoid going to screening, which will lower her risk by one-third"

- Dr. Peter C.Gøtzsche

Mammography has long been hailed as a critical tool for early detection of breast cancer, with the promise that it saves lives by catching cancers early. But recent studies and growing evidence suggest that mammograms may not be as effective—or as safe—as once believed. Let's delve into some surprising facts about mammography, backed by scientific studies, that might make you rethink this screening method.

The Promise vs. The Reality

The public narrative around mammography is straightforward: it catches cancer early, saves lives, and reduces the need for more aggressive treatments like mastectomies. However, the reality appears to be quite different. Several studies have raised significant concerns about the effectiveness of mammography screening in achieving these goals.

According to a review published in the *Journal of the Royal Society of Medicine*, if mammography screening were a drug, it likely would have been withdrawn from the market due to its unfavourable risk-benefit profile. The review argues that few, if any, women benefit from mammography, while many are harmed . In fact, the Swiss Medical Board has recommended discontinuing mammography screening altogether, and Switzerland has since banned it, citing more harm than good .

Over-diagnosis: The Elephant in the Room

One of the most significant issues with mammograms is over diagnosis. This occurs when mammography detects a cancer that would never have caused symptoms or become life-threatening. Over-diagnosis leads to unnecessary treatments, including surgery, radiation, and chemotherapy, all of which carry their own risks. A study published by the Nordic Cochrane Centre suggests that mammography produces breast cancer patients out of healthy women who would never have developed symptoms of breast cancer . Essentially, by avoiding mammography, a woman can significantly lower her risk of receiving a breast cancer diagnosis.

Mammograms Don't Seem to Save Lives

Despite the widespread belief that mammograms save lives by catching cancer early, data suggests otherwise. The Nordic Cochrane Centre, along with other major health organisations like the US and Canadian Task Forces and the Independent UK Panel, have found substantial problems with the randomised trials that initially supported mammography . These studies reveal no clear relationship between the start of screening and a reduction in breast cancer mortality. Moreover, the treatment of over-diagnosed cases —healthy women who are subjected to radiation, chemotherapy, or surgery—actually increases the risk of death from other causes, such as heart disease and secondary cancers caused by radiation .

The Problem of False Positives and False Negatives

Mammograms are also unreliable in terms of diagnostic accuracy. A false negative occurs when a mammogram fails to detect an existing tumor, giving a false sense of security. Conversely, a false positive happens when an abnormality is detected that appears to be cancer but is actually benign. Both scenarios have serious consequences: missed diagnoses in the first instance, and unnecessary anxiety, additional testing, and potentially harmful treatments in the second .

Radiation Risks: More Harm Than Good?

Another critical concern with mammography is the exposure to radiation. A study published in the *National Institutes of Health* journal found that annual mammography screening could induce 125 breast cancers per 100,000 women, leading to approximately 16 deaths . Women with larger breasts, who require additional imaging views, face even higher risks. For them, the rate of radiation-induced breast cancer and subsequent deaths is nearly double compared to women with smaller breasts. The study also indicates that switching to biennial screening starting at age 50 could reduce radiation-induced cancer risk by fivefold.

The Risks of Tumor Rupture

Beyond the issues of radiation and overdiagnosis, there's another hidden danger associated with mammograms: the risk of rupturing existing tumors. The mammogram process involves compressing the breast tissue between two plates, applying up to 42 pounds of pressure to ensure a clear image . However, studies have shown that as little as 22 pounds of pressure is enough to rupture the encapsulation of a cancerous tumor. This rupture can potentially spread malignant cells into the bloodstream, increasing the risk of metastasis, where cancer spreads to other parts of the body .

So, What Should Women Do?

Given the mounting evidence against routine mammography, it's crucial to approach breast cancer screening with a healthy dose of skepticism. Here are some considerations:

1. **Stay Informed:** Understand the risks and benefits of mammography and explore alternative screening methods, such as ultrasound or MRI, which may be safer and more effective in certain situations.

2. **Personalised Screening Plans:** Discuss with your healthcare provider about a screening plan tailored to your individual risk factors, such as family history, genetic predisposition, and breast density.

3. **Consider Less Frequent Screenings:** If you do opt for mammography, consider less frequent screenings, especially if you are at low to average risk for breast cancer.

4. **Focus on Prevention:** Adopt a healthy lifestyle that includes a balanced diet, regular exercise, and minimising exposure to known carcinogens. These steps can help reduce your overall cancer risk.

5. **Advocate for Better Screening Methods:** Encourage further research and advocate for the development and implementation of safer, more accurate breast cancer screening technologies.

Conclusion: A Serious Matter Deserves Serious Consideration

While the tone of this discussion may be a bit lighthearted, the topic is anything but. The potential dangers of mammography are significant, and it's essential for women to be fully informed about the risks and benefits before making decisions about their health. As the evidence continues to evolve, staying up-to-date with the latest research and maintaining an open dialogue with healthcare providers is the best strategy for navigating the complex landscape of breast cancer screening.

Chapter 6 - Smear Tests

"A result may be reported as positive even though there is no HPV infection or changes to cells of the cervix. This is called a 'false positive'. A false positive may mean you will have further tests that ultimately confirm there was no risk of cancer at that time. There are up to 62% of false positives every year. "

- Mark Schiffman, MD

Smear tests, represent a pivotal aspect of women's healthcare, aiming to detect abnormalities in cervical cells, particularly those linked to human papillomavirus (HPV) infections. Yet, delving deeper into the realm of HPV and cervical health unveils a tapestry of complexities and nuances often overlooked.

Understanding HPV

Human papillomavirus, comprising over 100 different types, with 14 identified as potentially cancerous, stands as one of the most prevalent infections worldwide. However, what's intriguing is the natural history of HPV infections—most cases resolve spontaneously within a few months to two years, without any intervention. Even the more concerning HPV strains, including those labeled high-risk, typically clear without evolving into cancerous conditions. It's essential to recognise that the mere presence of HPV cells doesn't inevitably translate into the development of cervical cancer. Instead, the immune system adeptly manages the majority of infections, preventing progression to malignancy.

The journey from HPV infection to cervical cancer unfolds over several years, with the progression typically taking 15 to 20 years in women with normal immune function and expedited to 5 to 10 years in those with compromised immunity. Hence, overreacting to HPV positivity can lead to unwarranted psychological distress and potential iatrogenic harm, emphasising the need for a balanced perspective.

Moreover, smear test results may yield false positives, indicating HPV infection or cervical cell changes that aren't indicative of imminent cancer risk. These false positives, prevalent in a **shocking** up to 62% of cases annually, may trigger unnecessary follow-up tests, subjecting individuals to heightened anxiety and additional medical procedures.

Ethylene Oxide

In understanding the substances involved in smear tests, attention turns to Ethylene Oxide, a chemical employed in the sterilisation of medical equipment. Ethylene oxide has been associated with various cancers, including lymphoma, leukemia, stomach, and breast cancers. The Environmental Protection Agency (EPA) has classified ethylene oxide as carcinogenic when inhaled, underscoring the importance of comprehending potential risks associated with medical procedures.

By unraveling the complexities surrounding smear tests, HPV infections, and associated risks, individuals can make informed decisions about their health, recognising the nuances beyond conventional narratives. Through knowledge empowerment and critical understanding, we pave the way for a more holistic approach to cervical health and well-being.

Alternative Methods

For those seeking a broader spectrum of HPV testing beyond conventional methods, alternative options are emerging to provide a more comprehensive assessment of cervical health. One such option is the urine sample HPV test, designed to detect a wider array of HPV strains compared to traditional screening protocols.

Unlike conventional smear tests, which typically focus on detecting a limited number of HPV strains, urine sample HPV tests offer a more expansive panel, targeting an extensive range of high-risk HPV types. This includes HPV 16, 18, 31, 59, 66, 53, 33, 58, 45, 56, 52, 35, 68, 51, 39, 82, 26, 73, 6, 11, and 81—almost four times the variety covered by standard NHS screenings.

By leveraging advanced testing methodologies, these alternative HPV tests aim to provide individuals with a more comprehensive assessment of their HPV status, empowering them with valuable insights into their cervical health. One such option available is the

HPV Type Home Test Kit, offering convenient and accessible testing solutions for individuals seeking enhanced HPV screening capabilities.

Through embracing alternative testing approaches, individuals can take proactive steps towards safeguarding their cervical health, gaining access to a more thorough evaluation of their HPV status. By expanding the scope of HPV testing beyond conventional parameters, these alternative options contribute to a more nuanced understanding of cervical health and facilitate informed decision-making regarding healthcare interventions.[iv]

[iv] https://medicinesonline.org.uk/product/hpv-type-home-test-kits/
https://www.gimaitaly.com/DocumentiGIMA/DocTecnici/st29702.pdf https://www.ncbi.nlm.nih.gov/pmc/articles/PMC6514435/
https://www.ncbi.nlm.nih.gov/pmc/articles/PMC6514435/

Chapter 7 - Vitamin K

"In order to absorb Vitamin K we have to have a functioning biliary and pancreas system. Your infant's digestive system isn't fully developed at birth which is why we give babies breast milk (and delay solids) until they are at least 6-months-old, and why breast milk only contains a small amount of highly absorbable Vitamin K"

When babies are born, they come equipped with special protective mechanisms, and one of these involves having lower levels of vitamin K compared to adults. This might sound concerning, but actually, it's quite beneficial and serves as a natural safeguard for newborns.

Firstly, babies are born with an immature digestive system, which means they can't process certain nutrients, including vitamin K, as efficiently as adults. Their tiny bodies need time to develop the ability to absorb and utilise nutrients properly. That's why breast milk, which contains a small amount of easily absorbable vitamin K, is recommended for the first few months.

Secondly, newborns receive a protective boost from stem cells present in cord blood. These stem cells help prevent bleeding and aid in repairing any damage inside the baby's body. To fully benefit from these stem cells, it's important to delay cord cutting and keep the blood thin so that the stem cells can travel easily and perform their vital functions.

Thirdly, newborns may have low levels of vitamin K because their intestines haven't yet been colonised by the bacteria necessary for synthesising it. Additionally, the "vitamin K cycle" isn't fully functional in newborns. While it might seem logical to administer vitamin K injections to bypass these issues, it's essential to remember that a baby's kidneys aren't fully developed either, raising concerns about how effectively their bodies can process the injected vitamin K.

Moreover, babies are born with lower vitamin K levels compared to adults, but this is usually enough to prevent any problems. Vitamin K injections are typically given to prevent Haemolytic Disease of the Newborn (HDN), which is so rare that it only occurs in 0.25-1.7% of cases.

In 1990 doctors researching the causes of childhood cancer studied some aspects of pregnancy and childbirth in two UK maternity hospitals. They found a higher risk of childhood cancer and Leukaemia in babies who had received vitamin K by injection.

Synthetic Vitamin K

Synthetic Vitamin K, also known as menadione, is used in the vitamin K injections for newborns. Unlike the natural vitamin K found in leafy greens and butter, menadione is not something you'll find in nature. What's more troubling is that it's not only more potent than natural vitamin K, but it's also associated with toxicity. This alarming fact is highlighted by the Food and Drug Administration's ban on menadione's use as an over-the-counter supplement due to its potential health risks.

Here's where things get concerning: synthetic vitamin K injections, is routinely administered to newborns without much consideration for the potential harm they may cause. Let's break it down further:

1. synthetic vitamin K shots don't actually contain any real vitamin K. Instead, they are loaded with a concoction of chemicals, including phenol (a poisonous acid found in coal tar), benzyl alcohol (a preservative), propylene glycol (commonly known as "edible" antifreeze), acetic acid (an agent used to kill microorganisms), hydrochloric acid, lecithin, and castor oil. It's quite alarming to think that these synthetic additives are being injected into vulnerable newborns.

2. synthetic vitamin K enthusiasts fail to grasp a fundamental concept: the reason why babies (and animals) have lower levels of vitamin K at birth. This lower level isn't a deficiency; it's a protective mechanism. Nature has designed it this way for a reason, yet we're quick to override it with synthetic interventions without fully understanding the implications.

In essence, the synthetic vitamin K used in injections poses significant risks to newborns, including potential toxicity and exposure to harmful additives. By shedding light on these facts, we hope to encourage a more informed dialogue about the use of synthetic vitamin K in newborn care and prompt parents to carefully consider the alternatives available. After all, our babies deserve nothing less than the safest and most natural start in life.[v]

---

[v] https://www.researchgate.net/publication/13761568_Case-control_studies_of_relation_between_childhood_cancer_and_neonatal_vitamin_K_administration
https://www.jstor.org/stable/29716562

Chapter 8 - Vaccines & Autism Link

"Autism has become so normalised that we forget it isn't normal."

Dr Andrew Wakefield & Autism.

Lets address the elephant in the room, shall we?

As soon as you mention Autism in the same sentence as vaccines, you will always see someone eye-roll. Dr Andrew Wakefield will be brought up and you will almost immediately get discredited as a 'crazy Anti-vaxxer' who knows nothing.

But, lets address some facts, shall we? Most people emoting the eye-roll do not actually have any idea on the truth of this history.

Dr. Andrew Wakefield was trained as a gastroenterologist. The basis for his now "debunked" (not true, by the way) clinical research paper in 1998 pointing to a possible link between the MMR (measles, mumps, rubella) vaccine and autism was that he biopsied the guts of a group of 12 autistic children and he found measles virus in the gastric mucosa. (Note: MMR is a live-virus vaccine.) Because of this, Dr. Wakefield, Prof. John Walker Smith, and Dr. Simon Burch (plus 10 co-authors) concluded there was sufficient reason for concern to merit further investigations.

"Onset of behavioural symptoms was associated, by the parents, with measles, mumps, and rubella vaccination in eight of the 12 children, with measles infection in one child, and otitis media in another. All 12 children had intestinal abnormalities, ranging from lymphoid nodular hyperplasia to aphthoid ulceration. Histology showed patchy chronic inflammation in the colon in 11 children and reactive ileal lymphoid hyperplasia in seven, but no granulomas. Behavioural disorders included autism (nine), disintegrative psychosis (one), and possible postviral or vaccinal encephalitis (two). There were no focal neurological abnormalities and MRI and EEG tests were normal. Abnormal laboratory results were significantly raised urinary methylmalonic acid compared with age-matched controls (p=0.003),

low haemoglobin in four children, and a low serum IgA in four children.

We identified associated gastrointestinal disease and developmental regression in a group of previously normal children, which was generally associated in time with possible environmental triggers."

Dr. Wakefield and his colleagues NEVER claimed a causal relationship between the MMR vaccine and autism. (They didn't do what the CDC has speedily done with Zika and microcephaly.) They simply acted responsibly as conscientious, caring physicians and reported what they had observed, and proceeded to recommend additional studies.

Now, separately, when Dr. Wakefield was asked in a news conference about his views on the MMR vaccine, what he said was that he thought the vaccine should be given separately. In other words, give the measles vaccine by itself rather than as part of the MMR combo. As a precautionary measure. Think about it. Makes sense, doesn't it? And for THAT, he was crucified. You see, the company (now GlaxoSmithKline) that produces the MMR vaccine in question feared that sales and usage of its product would plummet. The crucifixion was all based on pure market economics (and greed, of course).

So the firm used its significant political and media influence to go after Dr. Wakefield. (Hint: research the pharmaceutical industry interests of the Murdoch family (Rupert, James and all them), along with its ownership of the The Sunday Times of London, which published the series of hit pieces (by non-science contracted reporter Brian Deer) against Dr. Wakefield which ultimately destroyed his career.) Yes, you see, unlike Santa Claus and the Tooth Fairy, sometimes conspiracies are real.

In 2006, The Lancet, the worlds most prestigious medical journal wrote a public letter exonerating Dr Andrew Wakefield:

More than 6 years on, the original Lancet report should be viewed in the context of the emerging laboratory and clinical evidence of intestinal pathology, measles virus persistence in diseased tissues and abnormal measles immunity in this specific subset of children with autistic spectrum disorder. It would be inappropriate to interpret the events of the past month as exonerating MMR vaccine as a possible cause of autism.

Let us be clear that parents reported gastrointestinal symptoms in their children that many medical professionals denied and refused to investigate. Some parents were referred to social services and false claims of Munchausen's syndrome by proxy were levied. The parents were right; their children have an [vi]inflammatory intestinal disease. The medical profession was wrong, in some cases shamefully so. In light of this lesson it is imperative that rather than relying on endless reviews of epidemiological data which fail to even address the original hypothesis,4 parental claims should be taken seriously and their children should be investigated on an individual basis.

Vaccines & Autism Studies

http://www.ncbi.nlm.nih.gov/pmc/articles/PMC3878266/
http://www.ncbi.nlm.nih.gov/pubmed/21623535
http://www.ncbi.nlm.nih.gov/pubmed/25377033
http://www.ncbi.nlm.nih.gov/pubmed/24995277
http://www.ncbi.nlm.nih.gov/pubmed/12145534
http://www.ncbi.nlm.nih.gov/pubmed/21058170
http://www.ncbi.nlm.nih.gov/pubmed/22099159
http://www.ncbi.nlm.nih.gov/pmc/articles/PMC3364648/
http://www.ncbi.nlm.nih.gov/pubmed/17454560

[vi] [vi] https://childrenshealthdefense.org/wp-content/uploads/2016/11/Dr_BrianHooker_statement_regarding_Vaccine_Whistleblower_William_Thompson.pdf
https://www.thelancet.com/journals/lancet/article/PIIS0140-6736(04)15699-7/fulltext
https://www.researchgate.net/publication/5264909_A_statement_by_Dr_Andrew_Wakefield
https://pubmed.ncbi.nlm.nih.gov/9500320/

http://www.ncbi.nlm.nih.gov/pubmed/19106436
http://www.ncbi.nlm.nih.gov/pmc/articles/PMC3774468/
http://www.ncbi.nlm.nih.gov/pmc/articles/PMC3697751/
http://www.ncbi.nlm.nih.gov/pubmed/21299355
http://www.ncbi.nlm.nih.gov/pubmed/21907498
http://www.ncbi.nlm.nih.gov/pubmed/11339848
http://www.ncbi.nlm.nih.gov/pubmed/17674242
http://www.ncbi.nlm.nih.gov/pubmed/21993250
http://www.ncbi.nlm.nih.gov/pubmed/15780490
http://www.ncbi.nlm.nih.gov/pubmed/12933322
http://www.ncbi.nlm.nih.gov/pubmed/16870260
http://www.ncbi.nlm.nih.gov/pubmed/19043938
[vii]http://www.ncbi.nlm.nih.gov/pubmed/12142947
http://www.ncbi.nlm.nih.gov/pubmed/24675092

Causal relationship between vaccine induced immunity and autism

http://www.ncbi.nlm.nih.gov/pubmed/12849883

Subtle DNA changes and the overuse of vaccines in autism

http://www.ncbi.nlm.nih.gov/pmc/articles/PMC3364648/

Vaccine and Autism- a New Scientific Review

http://www.cbsnews.com/news/vaccines-and-autism-a-new-scientific-review/

Summary of previous Journal of Immunology

http://danmurphydc.com/wordpress/wp-content/uploads/2011/01/AR-10-12-rata-AUTISM-VACCINE.pdf

Autism and Resulting Medical Conditions:

http://www.tacanow.org/wp-content/uploads/2011/09/autism-studies-april-2008.pdf .

Mercury toxic encephalopathy manifesting with clinical symptoms of regressive autistic disorders. http://www.ncbi.nlm.nih.gov/pubmed/17454560

Relation of mercury to high autism rates in boys
http://www.ncbi.nlm.nih.gov/pubmed/16264412

Elevated levels of measles in children with Autism
http://www.ncbi.nlm.nih.gov/pubmed/12849883

Abnormal MMR antibodies in children with autism
http://www.ncbi.nlm.nih.gov/pubmed/12145534

Tylenol, MMR and Autism - A parent survey study
http://www.ncbi.nlm.nih.gov/pubmed/18445737

A Positive Association found between Autism Prevalence and Childhood Vaccination
http://www.ingentaconnect.com/content/tandf/uteh/2011/00000074/00000014/art00002?token=004c170388ee06a6e5865462431636f5720415d23763c247b5e4e26634a492f2530332976261

Peer reviewed study on fetal cell contamination with retro virus associated with autism and cancer
http://www.globalresearch.ca/new-study-in-journal-of-public-health-finds-autism-and-cancer-related-to-human-fetal-dna-in-vaccines/5402912

Study documentation- Dr Deisher

http://www.ms.academicjournals.org/article/article1409245960_Deisher%20et%20al.pdf

Autism and mercury poisoning
http://www.ncbi.nlm.nih.gov/pubmed/11339848

Hypothesis: conjugate vaccines may predispose children to autism spectrum disorders
http://www.ncbi.nlm.nih.gov/pubmed/21993250

Rise in autism coincides with rise in vaccines
http://www.ncbi.nlm.nih.gov/pubmed/21623535

A two-phase study evaluating the relationship between Thimerosal-containing vaccine administration and the risk for an autism spectrum disorder diagnosis in the United States
http://www.ncbi.nlm.nih.gov/pmc/articles/PMC3878266/

The study determined that autism could be a result from an atypical measles infection that produces neurological symptoms in some children. The source of this virus could be a variant of MV, or it could be the MMR vaccine.
http://www.ncbi.nlm.nih.gov/pubmed/12145534

Doctors who explain clearly why vaccines aren't safe or effective.

1. Dr. Nancy Banks - http://bit.ly/1Ip0aIm
2. Dr. Russell Blaylock - http://bit.ly/1BXxQZL
3. Dr. Shiv Chopra - http://bit.ly/1gdgh1s
4. Dr. Sherri Tenpenny - http://bit.ly/1MPVbjx

5. Dr. Suzanne Humphries - http://bit.ly/17sKDbf
6. Dr. Larry Palevsky - http://bit.ly/1LLEjf6
7. Dr. Toni Bark - http://bit.ly/1CYM9RB
8. Dr. Andrew Wakefield - http://bit.ly/1MuyNzo
9. Dr. Meryl Nass - http://bit.ly/1DGzJsc
10. Dr. Raymond Obomsawin - http://bit.ly/1G9ZXYl
11. Dr. Ghislaine Lanctot - http://bit.ly/1MrVeUL
12. Dr. Robert Rowen - http://bit.ly/1SIELeF
13. Dr. David Ayoub - http://bit.ly/1SIELve
14. Dr. Boyd Haley PhD - http://bit.ly/1KsdVby
15. Dr. Rashid Buttar - http://bit.ly/1gWOkL6
16. Dr. Roby Mitchell - http://bit.ly/1gdgEZU
17. Dr. Ken Stoller - http://bit.ly/1MPVqLI
18. Dr. Mayer Eisenstein - http://bit.ly/1LLEqHH
19. Dr. Frank Engley, PhD - http://bit.ly/1OHbLDI
20. Dr. David Davis - http://bit.ly/1gdgJwo
21. Dr Tetyana Obukhanych - http://bit.ly/16Z7k6J
22. Dr. Harold E Buttram - http://bit.ly/1Kru6Df
23. Dr. Kelly Brogan - http://bit.ly/1D31pfQ
24. Dr. RC Tent - http://bit.ly/1MPVwmu
25. Dr. Rebecca Carley - http://bit.ly/K49F4d
26. Dr. Andrew Moulden - http://bit.ly/1fwzKJu
27. Dr. Jack Wolfson - http://bit.ly/1wtPHRA
28. Dr. Michael Elice - http://bit.ly/1KsdpKA
29. Dr. Terry Wahls - http://bit.ly/1gWOBhd
30. Dr. Stephanie Seneff - http://bit.ly/1OtWxAY

Chapter 9 - Fluoride

"Fluoride is a neurotoxin - a toxic compound that specifically targets and affects neurones, causing neurological disorders and impairments. Studies show that fluoride can cross the blood-brain barrier and accumulate in the brain, leading to neurotoxic effects and impacting cognitive function - even causing IQ loss."

- Dr Eric Davis

The Alarming Truth about Fluoride

Fluoride, a substance often touted as a harmless additive to toothpaste and drinking water, is actually a potent neurotoxin that poses significant risks to human health. In fact, its toxic properties are comparable to those of arsenic, a known poison. Historically, fluoride was used as a rodenticide to kill rodents and continues to be used as a pesticide in some agricultural applications.

The Dangers of Fluoride Toxicity

Exposure to excessive levels of fluoride has been linked to a wide range of adverse health effects, including:

Cancer: Studies have linked fluoride exposure to an increased risk of cancer, particularly in the bladder, bone, and lung.

Cardiovascular disease: High levels of fluoride in the body have been linked to an increased risk of heart disease, high blood pressure and stroke.

Diabetes: Research suggests that fluoride may contribute to the development of insulin resistance and type 2 diabetes.

Thyroid disease: Fluoride has been shown to disrupt thyroid function, leading to hypothyroidism and other thyroid-related disorders.

Endocrine disruption: Exposure to fluoride has been linked to hormonal imbalances, affecting the development and function of the reproductive system.

Kidney disease: Prolonged fluoride exposure has been linked to kidney damage and increased risk of kidney disease.

Hypersensitivity: Some individuals may experience allergic reactions or hypersensitivity to fluoride, leading to skin rashes, itching, and other symptoms.

Reduced intelligence: Exposure to high levels of fluoride during fetal development and early childhood has been linked to reduced IQ and cognitive impairment.

Neurobehavioral deficits: Fluoride toxicity has been linked to changes in behaviour, mood, and cognitive function.
Visual impairment: High levels of fluoride have been linked to vision problems, including cataracts and glaucoma.

Arthritis: Some research suggests that fluoride exposure may contribute to the development of osteoarthritis and other joint-related disorders.

Nausea and other gastrointestinal symptoms: Fluoride toxicity can also cause gastrointestinal distress, including nausea, vomiting, and diarrhoea.

Every year, thousands of people, often children, turn to Poison Control Centres seeking help after ingesting excessive amounts of fluoride toothpaste and other fluoridated dental products. The most common symptoms of fluoride poisoning are gastrointestinal (GI) in nature, making it difficult for individuals to identify the source of their discomfort.

Fluoride Ingestion
Ingesting as little as 5 to 9 milligrams of fluoride can induce vomiting in children, according to a review of reports to Poison Control Centres in the United States. This alarming statistic highlights the potential dangers of fluoride exposure, particularly in young children who are more susceptible to its toxic effects.

The Compelling Evidence:
The scientific community has amassed a significant body of research highlighting the potential risks of fluoride exposure to brain health.

- The cumulative evidence from over 200 animal studies, 65 human studies, and numerous other investigations paints a concerning picture that when coupled with an iodine deficiency or aluminium excess, prolonged exposure to fluoride can lead to brain damage, as demonstrated by numerous animal studies.

- Moderately high fluoride exposures have also been linked to reduced intelligence in over 65 human studies, raising concerns about the potential long-term effects on cognitive development.

- Animal studies have consistently shown that fluoride can impair learning and memory capacity, with over 60 studies reporting this phenomenon.

- A total of 12 studies (7 human, 5 animal) have linked fluoride exposure to neurobehavioral deficits, including impaired visual-spatial organisation and other cognitive impairments.

- Three human studies have found that fluoride exposure during fetal development can lead to impaired brain development, potentially influencing the child's cognitive abilities.

- Seven Mother Offspring studies have investigated the relationship between fluoride levels in the urine of pregnant women and their offspring's IQ. These studies have consistently found that certain levels of fluoride exposure in pregnant women are linked to reduced IQ in their children.

The collective evidence from these studies suggests that fluoride exposure may have significant consequences for brain health, particularly during fetal development and early childhood.

The Lancet's Revelation:
In a groundbreaking review published in March 2014, The Lancet, a renowned medical journal, shed light on the alarming issue of

developmental neurotoxins. The study concluded that fluoride is one of only a few chemicals that has been proven to damage the developing brain. This devastating finding has far-reaching implications for the health and well-being of children worldwide.

How Fluoride's Toxicity Affects Children
Children are the most vulnerable to fluoride's toxic effects, and for good reason. Due to their small size, they are exposed to a larger dose of fluoride per pound of body weight than adults. In fact, infants can receive up to 400% more fluoride from fluoridated water than adults consuming the same amount. But, it's not just the amount of fluoride that's a concern. Children's kidneys are also less effective at excreting fluoride than adults. While healthy adults can excrete more than 50% of an ingested fluoride dose, infants can only manage to excrete 15 to 20%. This means that fluoride builds up in their bodies at a faster rate, leading to a higher risk of adverse health effects.

This is particularly concerning when it comes to infants fed formula made with fluoridated water. Studies have shown that these babies are more likely to suffer from dental fluorosis, a condition characterised by discolouration of the teeth caused by excessive fluoride ingestion during childhood.

There is no evidence whatsoever to state that fluoride is an essential nutrient. Unlike iodine, which is crucial for the proper functioning of the thyroid gland, fluoride is not necessary for human health. In fact, no human disease - including tooth decay - has been linked to a "deficiency" of fluoride.

Reducing Fluoride Exposure
Fortunately, reducing your fluoride intake is easier than you might think. Here are some simple steps to minimise your exposure and promote a healthier lifestyle:

1. **Ditch the Fluoridated Water**
The most obvious step is to switch to a non-fluoridated water source. Check with your local water utility to see if they offer fluoridated or non-fluoridated water options. If you're unsure, consider investing in a water filter that can remove fluoride from your drinking water.

2. **Choose Fluoride-Free Toothpaste**
When it comes to oral care, opt for fluoride-free toothpaste. Not only will this reduce your exposure to fluoride, but you'll also be giving your teeth a healthier start. Look for toothpaste that contains natural ingredients like essential oils and minerals instead.

3. **Skip the Fluoride Treatments**
When you visit the dentist, be sure to ask about fluoride-free treatment options. There are many alternative treatments that can help strengthen your teeth without exposing you to excessive fluoride.

4. **Cook Smart**
Non-stick pans may be convenient, but they can also leach fluoride into your food. Opt for cast iron or stainless steel pans instead, and avoid using non-stick pans at high heat.

5. **Monitor Your Exposure**
The best way to reduce fluoride exposure is to stay informed. Check the labels of your personal care products and food packaging for any signs of fluoride content. By being aware of your exposure, you can take proactive steps to minimise it.[viii]

[viii] https://www.ncbi.nlm.nih.gov/pmc/articles/PMC7261729/
https://fluoridealert.org/news/health-and-human-rights-top-anti-campaigners-lists/
https://fluoridealert.org/key-topics/health-effects-of-fluoride/

Chapter 10 - Breastfeeding

"Just like human blood, breast milk is a living fluid containing a range of germ killing substances, healthy bacteria, antibodies, white blood cells, antimicrobials and cell wall protectors and proteins that offer protection against bacteria and viruses. The live bacteria in Breast milk influences your baby's gut health – exclusive breastfeeding will colonise your baby's gut with healthy bacteria that may have life long benefits by helping develop resilience against conditions such as diabetes, obesity and metabolic syndrome."

I have an opinion on breastfeeding and formula that I believe is very unpopular. I believe that formula should only be available on prescription only…Hear me out.

Breastfeeding is HARD. Anyone who tells you it's easy is lyyyyinnnngggg or they were lucky. Breastfeeding when you have a job, is hard. Breastfeeding when you have other children, is hard. Breastfeeding when you have multiples is hard. Breastfeeding when you have depression, is hard. Breastfeeding when you have a preemie is hard… and SOME have all of the above.

I believe that breastfeeding should be seen as an extension of pregnancy. You don't drink alcohol or smoke when you're pregnant because you know it's just not the done thing. They tell you not to eat certain foods, you anticipate how uncomfortable the pregnancy can be, you know it'll get painful, you know it'll be hard… but it's expected as it's part of growing your child. Breastfeeding is the same. There is NO comparison between formula and breastmilk, none. Breastmilk is far more superior and changes every single time your child feeds. It can change colour too! If your child is unwell, your body will create more hind milk that contains more antibodies in it to nurture your child. It contains a crazy amount of natural antibodies to fight off infections, bugs and other ailments. Breastfed babies have a lower risk of asthma, obesity, type 1 diabetes, and sudden infant death syndrome (SIDS). Breastfed babies are also less likely to have ear infections and stomach bugs. Not only that, but mothers who breastfeed have a lower risk of breast cancer, post natal depression and type 2 diabetes.

Unfortunately, there is very little help for mothers who are struggling with breastfeeding. They may check if your baby has a tongue tie at birth, but they're not experienced in posterior tongue ties that can not be seen and only felt/analysed. They may recommend nipple shields or give you some nipple cream…OR a health visitor might come out later and tell you that your baby just isn't happy, so, formula feed!

I remember feeding my Son and I would CRY before every single feed for the anticipation as it was AGONY. And I mean, agonising. I had the midwife check him, I had nipple shields, I had everyone telling me that it's not normal for it to hurt, I had a breastfeeding specialist see him and say he was fine and THEN I paid privately for a lactation consultant and low and behold, he was tongue tied. This wasn't rectified until he was 5 months old, by this time my nipples were bleeding, cracked and completely destroyed, even a t-shirt touching them would hurt me. But, I persisted. I had every health professional going tell me that my mental health came first, that I mattered more, that formula was just as good… but I knew that was a lie.

With my youngest, breastfeeding a 26 week old baby and having to express every hour…. That really tested my testament, BUT I did it and she's never had a drop of formula, despite me literally having to battle the head of NICU as he was trying to force me to use formula… I was depressed as fuck, but I fought.

What I'm trying to say is that I KNOW how hard it is, I know what a shit journey it can be… but we are mothers, it's what we are biologically meant to be doing. Less than 2% of women worldwide physically can't breastfeed, the rest, I believe is a lack of education, a lack of want and pressure from 'health professionals.' Keep in mind, the NHS get funding from formula companies…. They get nothing when you breastfeed.

If formula was only available on prescription, the whole thing would be seen differently. Donor milk would be a lot more widely accepted, I accepted donor milk with all of my pregnancies and relied on it heavily with my youngest towards the end. To the people saying there isn't much available, rubbish. I was inundated with requests after using websites and donor milk pages online. Every hospital also has its own donor milk bank and they have them privately too. It wouldn't be frowned upon like it is now and I believe wet nursing would come back. I've had friends of mine feed my babies when they were little when they were being looked after by them and they wouldn't take a bottle. How that is frowned upon more so than giving them the poisons of formula, I do not know. Breasts were made for babies. The milk is made for babies. I believe there would be websites that would do milk deliveries and this would be wildly accepted.

If formula was available on prescription only, there would be a lot less babies with colic, food allergies, skin issues and gut and bowel issues. If formula was available on prescription only, the NHS and birthing centres would be FORCED to train their staff adequately to give the correct help to mothers. They would have lactation consultants and lactation advisors to hand. They would explain the benefits of pumping vs doing it too early. They would let you know that just because you breastfeed, it doesn't mean your partner can't be involved. They would tell you that you can still breastfeed on the medication you are on and they would eradicate all the misinformation around that. They would be forced to help mothers with mastitis, thrush, tongue tie. They would fix the issues that arise instead of easily palming them off with 'you can't breastfeed'.

If formula was available on prescription only, there would be a lot less babies with colic, food allergies, skin issues and gut and bowel issues. If formula was available on prescription only, the NHS and birthing centres would be FORCED to train their staff adequately to give the correct help to mothers. They would have lactation consultants and lactation advisors to hand. They would explain the benefits of pumping vs doing it too early. They would let you know that just because you breastfeed, it doesn't mean your partner can't be involved. They would tell you that you can still breastfeed on the medication you are on and they would eradicate all the misinformation around that. They would be forced to help mothers with mastitis, thrush, tongue tie. They would fix the issues that arise instead of easily palming them off with 'you can't breastfeed'.

If formula was on a prescription only basis, I believe we would have much healthier babies, healthier children and it would become normalised just as much as pregnancy is. Formula is no where near the expectation of breastfeeding and I'm sorry but if you're going to say 'fed is best' - no. Fed is the BARE MINIMUM that is expected. Breast is best.[ix]

[ix] https://milkbankne.org/2023/08/breastmilk-11-fascinating-facts/
https://www.nuffieldtrust.org.uk/resource/breastfeeding
https://anya.health/breastfeeding-uk/
https://stateofchildhealth.rcpch.ac.uk/evidence/maternal-perinatal-health/breastfeeding/
https://www.bda.uk.com/resource/breastfeeding.html

Chapter 11 - Natural Remedies & Treatments

"For every human illness, somewhere in the world there exists a plant which is the cure."

- Rudolf Steiner

As we navigate the complexities of modern healthcare, it's easy to get caught up in the hype surrounding pharmaceuticals and medical treatments. We're often led to believe that the only way to alleviate our symptoms and treat our ailments is through a pill or a prescription. But what if I told you that there's a more effective, more natural, and more empowering way to take care of your body?

Nature has been providing us with remedies and cures for thousands of years, long before the advent of modern medicine. From ancient civilisations like the Egyptians and the Greeks to modern-day herbalists and naturopaths, humans have been harnessing the power of plants, minerals, and other natural elements to heal and protect our bodies.

So, why do we often ignore our bodies' natural instincts and turn instead to synthetic solutions? One reason, is that we've been conditioned to believe that our bodies are flawed and in need of correction. If we believe that we are unable to heal ourselves, then we are forever a slave to the pharmaceutical world…If we can heal ourselves, then they have lost 7 billion customers.

We're told that our bodies are prone to disease and decay and that we need to take medications to prevent these problems. But what if our bodies are actually designed to be healthy and resilient, and that we just need to learn how to trust them? When we trust our bodies, we begin to listen to their innate wisdom. We start to recognise that our bodies are capable of healing themselves, and that we don't need to rely on external interventions to stay healthy. This is especially important for women, who are often socialised to prioritise others' needs over their own physical and emotional well-being.

My Favourite Homeopathic Remedies

1 - Arnica montana (Arnica):

Arnica is a well-known homeopathic remedy often used for injuries, bruising, and trauma as well as sprains, muscle aches, wound healing, superficial phlebitis, joint pain, inflammation from insect bites and swelling from broken bones. It's believed to reduce inflammation and promote the body's natural healing processes. Arnica is commonly used topically in the form of gels or creams.

2 - Chamomilla (Chamomile)

Chamomile is recognised for its calming properties and is often used in homeopathy to address conditions related to irritability, teething in infants, digestive upset, hay fever, inflammation, muscle spasms, menstrual disorders, insomnia, ulcers, wounds, gastrointestinal disorders, rheumatic pain, and haemorrhoids. Essential oils of chamomile are used extensively in cosmetics and aromatherapy.It can be taken orally or applied topically.

3 - Ignatia amara (Ignatia)

Ignatia is often employed for emotional distress, particularly grief, and is commonly used after the shock of a loss. It's believed to help ease emotional pain and promote emotional balance. It is one of the homeopathic remedies most commonly used on patients with anxiety symptoms, depression, manic episodes, emotive urination and diarrhoea, as well as hyperaesthesia and hypersensitivity to emotions. It is also one of the first remedies to have been formally studied in laboratory animals to use as medicine.

4 - Nux vomica (Nux Vom)

Nux vomica is frequently recommended for individuals experiencing digestive issues, especially after overindulgence in food or stimulants as well as indigestion, heartburn, constipation, and nausea. It's thought to support the body in detoxifying and restoring balance.

5 - Rhus toxicodendron (Rhus Tox)

Rhus tox is a common remedy for conditions involving stiffness and pain that improve with movement. It is often used for arthritis, strains, and sprains, and is believed to provide relief from discomfort due to anti inflammatory agents. It also has dual benefits and works well with skin irritations, rheumatic pains, mucous membrane afflictions, and typhoid type fever.

6 - Aconitum napellus (Aconite)

Aconite is often used in the early stages of an illness, particularly when symptoms come on suddenly like cold or flu, exposure to dry, cold weather or very hot weather; tingling, coldness, and numbness; influenza or colds with congestion; and heavy, pulsating headaches.

7 - Gelsemium sempervirens (Gelsemium)

Gelsemium is a remedy made from the root of the yellow jasmine plant. It is often associated with feelings of weakness, fatigue, and heaviness. It is commonly used for symptoms related to flu, such as muscle aches and a heavy, droopy feeling.

8 - Atropa Belladonna (Belladonna)

While it has been used as a poison in the past, scientists today extract chemicals from belladonna for use in medicine. In its homeopathic form is not toxic at all and quite the opposite. It is recognised for its amazing ability to help address sudden and intense symptoms like fever and inflammation, ear infections, throbbing headaches, respiratory distress, teething troubles, skin conditions and much more.

9 - Rescue Remedy

Rescue Remedy, manufactured by Nelsons, contains five flower essences - Rock Rose to alleviate terror and panic, Impatiens to mollify irritation and impatience, ClematisStar of Bethlehem to ease shock, and Cherry Plum to calm irrational thoughts.

10 - St Johns Wart

John's wort may be used for nerve pain (neuralgia), anxiety, and tension. It may also aid in weakness, stress, irritability, and sleeping issues (insomnia). It's also claimed to ease the pain due to some conditions. These include sciatica, rheumatoid arthritis, and menstruation.

Teething (Babies)

- Amber Teething Necklace
- Helios (ABC) Remedy
- Teething Granules (Teetha)
- Belladonna
- Breast Milk

Conjunctivitis

- The best remedy is breast milk, but Golden Eye Conjunctivitis Ointment and warm tea bags to clean the eye are also effective.
- Apis Mel (Helios) can also be used.

Stings

- For wasp or bee stings, drench the area in apple cider vinegar immediately.
- Cover with baking soda or toothpaste, then put a plaster over it for an hour.
- After that, use arnica cream and leave it uncovered.
- Apis Mellifica (Helios) and/or Hypericum (Helios) are also recommended.

Sinusitis

- Use slippery elm for all forms and have a humidifier in the room with 5 drops of colloidal silver.
  Frontal Sinusitis (above the brow with light sensitivity):

- Arsenicum or Nux Vomica

- Maxillary Sinusitis (beneath the eyes with tooth pain): Calc Carb or Pulsatilla

- Ethmoid Sinusitis (pain and pressure behind the eyes): Silicea, Ferrum Phos, and Belladonna

Tonsillitis/Sore Throat

- Belladonna (for pain and anti-inflammatory), raw honey, elderberry syrup, and colloidal silver (3 sprays in the throat, 3 times a day).

Ear Ache/Infections

- Belladonna, Aconite, and Pulsatilla (all in the Helios first aid box and all treat ear infections).
- Garlic oil: put two or three drops of warm garlic oil into the ear (Neal's Yard Mullen Garlic Oil is recommended).

Vomiting

- Drink plenty of water, even if it comes back up.
- Activated charcoal tablets (recommended: Oceans Alive Health), ashwagandha, Bryonia (Helios) or Argentum (Helios), and ginger biscuits (without sweeteners).

Tooth Pain (Adults)

- Salt water rinse (mix 1/2 teaspoon of salt into a glass of warm water and gargle).
- Peppermint tea bags (press onto the affected area).
- Garlic: crush a garlic clove to create a paste (you can also add salt) and apply to the area, or chew a clove of fresh garlic.
- Remedies to try: Silicea, Plantago, Merc Sol.

Urine Infection/Discomfort

- D-Mannose is a must-have in the cupboard; it works within hours.
- Drink a pint glass of organic cranberry juice.
- Staphysagria and Belladonna for pain and discomfort.

Treatments

Measles treatment

Vitamin A: Give 200,000 IU per day for two days only.
For a healthy baby: 5,000 IU.

For general support: A, 40,000 IU (16 drops) per day, spread out over the day for two days.

Comfort and Environment: Keep the child in a dimly lit room and ensure they stay warm. Avoid allowing them to catch a chill, as this can lead to complications.
Ensure they have plenty of fluids, starting with water and gradually introducing fruit juices and herbal teas like Rosehip and Elderberry.Minimise food intake to conserve energy for healing. Fasting allows the body to rest, so start feeding again once the fever has subsided.

Immune Support: Boost the immune system with supplements such as Vitamin C, Vitamin D, Zinc, Garlic, and Echinacea.

Rash Relief: Soothe the rash by bathing the child with 3 tablespoons of baking soda or porridge oats in the bath. Chamomile, Calendula, Bach Rescue Cream, and Aloe Vera can also provide relief.

Eye Care: Avoid bright light and bathe the eyes with Euphrasia (Eyebright). Sensitivity to light can persist for 1 to 5 weeks after the fever.

Distress Relief: Use Lavender oil on a pillow or Bach's Rescue Remedy to calm the child.

Fever Management

Normal Fever: A typical body temperature is 37°C. Children and adults can handle fevers up to 40°C for several days without danger. Healthy children often experience high fevers of 39.5°C or higher during infections.

High Fever Concern: A temperature of 40.5°C is worrisome, and temperatures above 41°C can be life-threatening. Regularly administer Aconite, Belladonna, or Chamomilia, but avoid Aspirin.

Homeopathic Remedies:
- Aconite: For high fever with pale skin.
- Belladonna: For high fever with a red face and eye inflammation.
- Stramonium: For high fever with a red face and convulsions.
- Euphrasia: For eye inflammation.
- Pulsatilla: For diarrhoea, yellow discharge, cough, clinginess, and eye inflammation.
- Bryonia: For a hard, painful cough, high temperature, and thirst.

MUMPS

Diet:

- Both adults and children should stick to soft foods until they feel better and the swelling decreases.
- Ensure children get plenty of fluids to stay hydrated.

Supplements:

- **Probiotic Supplement:** Choose one containing Lactobacillus acidophilus to help maintain intestinal health and potentially strengthen the immune system.

- **Bromelain:** This enzyme from pineapple, taken between meals, can reduce inflammation. It's often used with turmeric (Curcuma longa), an anti-inflammatory that enhances bromelain's effects.

Recommended Herbs:

- **Green Tea (Camellia sinensis):** An antioxidant that may boost the immune system. Use caffeine-free products. You can also prepare teas from the herb's leaves.

- **Elderberry (Sambucus nigra):** Extract has antiviral properties and may strengthen the immune system. Consult a healthcare provider before giving it to a child. Pregnant or breastfeeding women, or individuals with autoimmune diseases or on immunosuppressive drugs, should avoid elderberry.

Common Homeopathic Remedies for Mumps:

- **Aconitum:** For childhood illnesses like mumps, especially with sudden onset and fever.
- **Belladonna:** Commonly used for mumps, particularly with rapid onset.
- **Mercurius:** For mumps with swelling worse on the right side, excessive foul-smelling perspiration, and salivation.
- **Phytolacca:** For mumps where glands feel swollen and hard.
- **Pilocarpinum:** For mumps with excessive perspiration and salivation, and considerable thirst. Some homeopaths consider this the best remedy for mumps.
- **Pulsatilla:** For later stages of mumps, especially in adolescents.
- **Rhus toxicodendron:** For mumps with swelling worse on the left side.

Environment:

- Keep the child in a quiet, dimly lit room, ensuring they stay warm to avoid chills, which can lead to complications.

Hydration:

- Provide plenty of fluids, starting with water and then introducing fruit juices and herbal teas like Rosehip and Elderberry.

Diet:

- Minimise food intake to conserve energy for healing. Start feeding again once the fever has subsided.

Swelling Relief:

- Apply cold compresses to the swollen areas (cheeks and jaw) to reduce discomfort and swelling. Chamomile, Calendula, and Aloe Vera can also help soothe the skin.

Mouth Care:

- Rinse the mouth with warm salt water to maintain oral hygiene and reduce discomfort.
- Avoid acidic foods and drinks that can irritate the swollen glands.

Distress Relief:

- Use Lavender oil on a pillow or Bach's Rescue Remedy to calm the child.

Whooping Cough

Nutrition and Supplements

Diet:

- Provide small, frequent meals consisting of vegetable broths, steamed vegetables, and fresh fruits.
- Ensure children get plenty of fluids.
-

Supplements:

- **Vitamin C, Zinc, and Beta-Carotene:** Use beta-carotene instead of vitamin A.

Common Homeopathic Remedies for Whooping Cough:

- **Antimonium Tartaricum:** For rattling in the chest with a strong, loose cough. The child is weak and has difficulty bringing up phlegm, often bending backward while coughing and feeling sleepy after coughing fits. Symptoms include shortness of breath, a sense of suffocation, and feeling better sitting up. The cough can end in vomiting, and the child is irritable and prefers to be left alone.
- **Coccus Cacti:** For winter coughs with clear, thick, ropey mucus. The child feels better in cold air and drinking cold

liquids. Coughing fits can end in choking and vomiting, often occurring from 6-7 a.m. and after 11:30 p.m.
- **Cuprum:** For violent coughing fits causing cyanosis (turning blue). Associated with spasms and cramps, and the child desires cold drinks and to lie down.
- **Drosera:** For violent coughing spells ending in choking, gagging, or vomiting. Worse when lying down and after midnight. Symptoms include a barking cough, throat dryness, tickling, bloody nose, and hoarse voice.
- **Ipecacuanha:** For severe suffocative coughs ending in retching, vomiting, or cyanosis. Symptoms include nausea, aversion to food, rattling in the chest, and a bloody nose. The cough is worse at 7 p.m. and better in fresh air.
- **Bryonia:** For dry, painful coughs made worse by movement and better by being still. Symptoms include holding the chest while coughing, worsening with eating and drinking, and irritability. The cough often worsens at 9 p.m.
- **Pertussin:** For dry, choking, hacking coughs triggered by a tickle in the throat or chest. The cough is deep, croupy, and accompanied by flushed face and sighing at the end of an attack. Can be used as an immune strengthener during outbreaks.

Immune-Boosting Herbs

- Echinacea (Echinacea purpurea):
- Garlic (Allium sativum):
- Astragalus (Astragalus membranaceus):
- Expectorants (Help Get Rid of Mucus)
- Hyssop (Hyssopus officinalis):
- Anise (Pimpinella anisum):
- Elecampane (Inula helenium):
- Mullein (Verbascum densiflorum):

- Antispasmodic Herbs
- Indian Tobacco (Lobelia inflata):
- Catnip (Nepeta cataria):
- Chamomile (Matricaria recutita):

General Care and Comfort

Environment:

- Keep the child in a quiet, comfortable environment with plenty of rest.

Hydration:

- Ensure the child drinks plenty of fluids, including water, fruit juices, and herbal teas.

Diet:

- Offer small, frequent meals of soft foods like vegetable broths, steamed vegetables, and fresh fruits.

Comfort:

- Use cold compresses to relieve chest discomfort.
- Keep the child in a well-ventilated room with fresh air.
- Elevate the child's head during sleep to ease breathing.

Rubella/German Measles

- Antioxidant vitamins A, C, E, D, B-complex vitamins, and trace minerals (magnesium, calcium, zinc, selenium).
- **Purpose:** Supports overall health and immune function.

Herbs

Herbs can help strengthen the immune system and reduce symptoms. Always consult a healthcare provider before giving herbs to a child.

1. **Rhodiola (Rhodiola rosea):**

    - **Dosage:** 150 to 300 mg, 1 to 3 times daily.
    - **Purpose:** Immune support and stress adaptation.

2. **Cat's Claw (Uncaria tomentosa):**

    - **Dosage:** 20 mg, 3 times daily.
    - **Purpose:** Reduces inflammation and stimulates the immune system.

3. **Reishi Mushroom (Ganoderma lucidum):**

    - **Dosage:** 150 to 300 mg, 2 to 3 times daily or 30 to 60 drops of tincture, 2 to 3 times daily.
    - **Purpose:** Reduces inflammation and boosts immunity.

Homeopathy

1. Aconitum: Use: Sudden fever, rash, and thirst.

2. Belladonna: Use: Sudden onset rubella with high fever, flushed face, and radiating heat. Suitable for minimal perspiration and strange dreams.

3. Ferrum Phosphoricum: Use: Early-stage rubella with mild-to-moderate fever and tiredness.

4. Pulsatilla: Use: Fever and chills worsened in warm rooms and improved in fresh air. Symptoms are generally less intense.

Tetanus

Tetanus is a bacterial infection that originates from the feces of farmyard animals.

The tetanus bacteria are anaerobic, meaning they cannot survive in the presence of oxygen. Therefore, if a wound bleeds, there is no chance of developing tetanus. It typically takes 2-3 weeks for the body to develop antibodies from the supposed vaccine, therefore it would be completely pointless to use that as a precautionary measure as it wouldn't have time to activate any antibodies. It is also very important to note that the tetanus vaccine is not just that, it is a 3-in-1 booster for Tetanus, Diptheria and Pertusis - it is not a vaccine to prevent, it even states that it doesn't claim to prevent transmission, just 'lessen symptoms'.

There is a tetanus antitoxin called immunoglobulin that can be used within 24 hours if necessary. However, it also takes 1-2 weeks for the body to develop antibodies in response to this treatment. So, again, pointless.

If Tetanus is present, antibiotics are used.

Chapter 12 - Suncream

"The sun is not our enemy. For Generations, it has been the treatment for low moods, auto-immune diseases and illnesses. Why now has it suddenly been demonised?"

The Truth About Suncream and Sun Exposure

Many people are intrigued by the idea of foregoing sunscreen, so let me delve deeper into this topic.

It's one of the most pervasive misconceptions ever perpetuated. How does one ensure a perpetual profit? By convincing people that something vital for life is actually harmful. The notion that "the sun causes cancer" has been ingrained in our minds, yet emerging evidence suggests that certain sunscreens may pose risks.

We inhabit a planet where sunlight is essential for our well-being. Sunlight is the primary natural source of vitamin D, crucial for bone health, immune function, and overall vitality. It seems counterintuitive that the same sun that sustains life could also be inherently detrimental.

Our skin, the body's largest organ, acts as a formidable barrier against environmental elements. However, many conventional sunscreens contain chemical filters such as avobenzone, oxybenzone, octocrylene, homosalate, octisalate, and octinoxate. These chemicals have been identified as potential endocrine disruptors and carcinogens. Despite this, the promotion of sunscreen is vigorously championed by industries citing sun exposure as a primary cause of skin cancer. Increasingly, scientists and medical professionals are challenging this narrative, suggesting that sunscreen ingredients may be more harmful than the sun itself.

Sunscreen use can inhibit the skin's ability to synthesise vitamin D. Studies indicate that sunscreen with high SPF values and frequent application can significantly reduce vitamin D production. Ironically, even with diligent sunscreen application, individuals may still experience vitamin D deficiency, which is associated with increased risks of various cancers and chronic diseases.

Moreover, sunscreen chemicals can interfere with the body's production of vitamin E, a vital antioxidant that supports skin health and protects against UV damage. This interference can disrupt the skin's natural ability to develop melanin, the pigment responsible for shielding against sunburns. Some individuals report increased sunburns while using sunscreen, as the chemicals and UV-blocking agents can prevent the skin from adapting and building natural defences against UV rays.

Mainstream sunscreens often contain aluminium compounds, which can further sensitive the skin and exacerbate sun-related skin issues. The absorption of these chemicals into the bloodstream raises concerns about potential long-term health effects.

If you opt to use sunscreen, consider choosing organic, mineral-based formulas that use zinc oxide or titanium dioxide as active ingredients. These ingredients provide effective broad-spectrum protection without penetrating the skin or disrupting bodily functions. Mineral sunscreens sit on the skin's surface, reflecting and scattering UV rays without causing harm.

It's essential to avoid high SPF sunscreens (above SPF 50), as they offer minimal additional protection while potentially increasing exposure to harmful chemicals. Instead, prioritise frequent reapplication of lower SPF sunscreens, combined with protective clothing and seeking shade during peak sun hours, to minimise exposure risks.

For those transitioning away from habitual sunscreen use, gradual exposure to sunlight is key. This approach allows the skin to acclimate and naturally increase its resistance to UV rays. My own children, for example, have traveled to tropical regions during scorching summer months with temperatures exceeding 40 degrees Celsius, relying on gradual sun exposure without conventional sunscreens, and have not experienced sunburn.

Our bodies tan for a reason; it's a natural defence mechanism evolved over millennia to protect against UV damage. The sun, when enjoyed responsibly, offers profound health benefits beyond vitamin D production, including mood enhancement, immune support, and skin health.

Let's not allow profit-driven agendas to distort our understanding of sun exposure. The sun is not our enemy; it's a vital source of life and well-being that deserves respect and moderation in our approach.

Additional Considerations:

It's worth noting that wearing sunglasses, while shielding the eyes from UV rays, can affect the body's internal clock. UV exposure through the eyes helps regulate the production of melatonin and vitamin D, crucial for maintaining circadian rhythms and overall health. Consider balancing sun exposure to both skin and eyes for optimal health benefits.

By educating ourselves and making informed choices about sun exposure and sunscreen use, we can safeguard our health while embracing the natural benefits of sunlight responsibly.

Choosing Safer Alternatives

If you opt to use sunscreen, consider choosing organic, mineral-based formulas that use zinc oxide or titanium dioxide as active ingredients. These ingredients provide effective broad-spectrum protection without penetrating the skin or disrupting bodily functions. Mineral sunscreens sit on the skin's surface, reflecting and scattering UV rays without causing harm. Non-nano zinc oxide is particularly recommended as it does not get absorbed into the skin and remains effective without the potential risks associated with nano-sized particles.

Safe Sun Exposure Practices

It's essential to avoid high SPF sunscreens (above SPF 30), as they offer minimal additional protection while potentially increasing exposure to harmful chemicals. Instead, prioritise frequent reapplication of lower SPF sunscreens, combined with protective clothing and seeking shade during peak sun hours, to minimise exposure risks.

For those transitioning away from habitual sunscreen use, gradual exposure to sunlight is key. This approach allows the skin to acclimate and naturally increase its resistance to UV rays. Training your skin in the spring sun, autumn sun, and early morning or evening sun is an effective way to build tolerance and maximise vitamin D synthesis while minimising the risk of sunburn.

Protecting Children

Children should wear SPF/UV-protected clothing during peak sun times if direct exposure cannot be avoided. It's advisable to keep children out of intense sunlight if they have not acclimated their skin gradually over time. Balancing outdoor activities with sun protection measures ensures their health and well-being while enjoying the benefits of sunlight responsibly.

x

---

x

https://jamanetwork.com/journals/jama/article-abstract/2759002?guestAccessKey=81a4a1e1-66d2-4f85-8d80-8d4d1aa1c56e&utm_source=For_The_Media&utm_medium=referral&utm_campaign=ftm_links&utm_content=tfl&utm_term=012120

https://www.google.co.uk/amp/s/medicalxpress.com/news/2019-05-sunscreen-chemicals-bloodstream-potentially-unsafe.amp

https://www.ewg.org/sunscreen/report/the-trouble-with-sunscreen-chemicals/

https://thetruthaboutcancer.com/causes-of-skin-cancer/

https://www.webmd.com/skin-problems-and-treatments/news/20200121/fda-skin-absorbs-dangerous-sunscreen-chemicals

https://www.health.com/condition/skin-cancer/fda-sunscreen-warning

https://naturalsociety.com/sunscreen-causes-cancer-what-you-may-not-know-about-sunscreen/

https://www.collective-evolution.com/2017/02/13/how-sunscreen-could-be-causing-skin-cancer-not-the-sun/

Chapter 13 - Microwaves

"After some 20 years of research into their use, Soviet Russia banned the use of microwave ovens for heating food in 1976 as they decided that the dangers outweighed the benefit of speed."

Microwaving prepared meats sufficiently to insure sanitary ingestion caused formation of d-Nitrosodienthanolamines, a well-known carcinogen. Microwaving milk and cereal grains converted some of their amino acids into carcinogens. Thawing frozen fruits converted their glucoside and galactoside containing fractions into carcinogenic substances. Extremely short exposure of raw, cooked or frozen vegetables converted their plant alkaloids into carcinogens. Carcinogenic free radicals were formed in microwaved plants, especially root vegetables. Some Russian researchers, in their studies of the changes in food quality when it is cooked in a microwave oven, have reported a marked acceleration of structural degradation leading to a decreased food value of 60 to 90% in all foods tested. They found significant decreases in the bio-availability of B complex vitamins, vitamin C, vitamin E, essential minerals and lipotropins (substances that prevent abnormal accumulation of fat). This was confirmed in a Japanese study when they found that approximately 30-40% of vitamin B12 was lost in foods cooked by microwaves (Watanabe 1998). B12 deficiency is one of several factors that can cause dementia.

A clinical study done by Dr HV Hertel and Dr BH Blanc of the Swiss Federal Institute of Technology tells volumes: The small, but well-controlled study showed the significant degeneration of nutrients produced in microwaved foods. The conclusion showed that microwave cooking produced adverse changes in human blood. In intervals of two to five days, the volunteers in the study received one of the following food variants on an empty stomach:

- raw milk;
- the same milk conventionally cooked;
- pasteurised milk;
- the same raw milk cooked in a microwave oven;
- raw vegetables from an organic farm;
- the same vegetables cooked conventionally;
- the same vegetables frozen and defrosted in a microwave oven;

- the same vegetables cooked in the microwave oven.

Once the volunteers were isolated, blood samples were taken from every volunteer immediately before eating.
Then, blood samples were taken at defined intervals after eating of the above milk or vegetable preparations.

Significant changes were discovered in the blood samples from the intervals following the foods cooked in the microwave oven. These changes included a decrease in all haemoglobin and cholesterol values, especially the ratio of HIDL (good cholesterol) and LDL (bad cholesterol) values.

Carcinogens were formed in virtually all foods tested. No test food was subjected to more microwaving than necessary to accomplish the purpose, i.e., cooking, thawing, or heating to insure sanitary ingestion.

Additionally, there was a highly significant association between the amount of microwave energy in the test foods and the luminous power of luminescent bacteria exposed to serum from test persons who ate that food.

Chapter 14 - Sunbeds

"...The data revealed a notable 23 percent decrease in deaths attributed to cardiovascular diseases among sunbed users compared to non-users."

Recent research has significantly reshaped the narrative around sunbed use, highlighting a range of potential health benefits that challenge the traditional perceptions of UV exposure.

A large-scale study, for instance, tracked sunbed use and the health outcomes of approximately 395,000 white participants aged 37 to 73 over an average follow-up period of 12.7 years. The findings were striking: those who regularly used sunbeds experienced a 15 percent reduction in overall mortality during the study period. Even more remarkable, the risk of death from cardiovascular diseases was reduced by 23 percent, and the likelihood of dying from cancer decreased by 14 percent among sunbed users compared to non-users.

These results are not isolated. A growing body of evidence supports the health benefits associated with moderate sunbed use. Many independent studies have shown that regular exposure to sunbeds can lead to significant improvements in health, particularly in boosting essential vitamin levels. For example, one study demonstrated that using a sunbed for just five minutes once a week could substantially increase levels of vitamins C, D, and E. These vitamins play a critical role in maintaining a healthy immune system, supporting cardiovascular health, and improving overall mental well-being.

One particular study involved 50 participants who were all vitamin D deficient at the outset. During the study, 20 of these participants used a sunbed for the recommended five minutes per week over a six-week period. Remarkably, by the end of the study, only the 30 participants who did not use the sunbed remained vitamin D deficient. This finding underscores the potential of sunbeds to effectively boost vitamin D levels, which is particularly significant given the widespread prevalence of vitamin D deficiency and its association with a range of health issues, including weakened immune function, bone disorders, and increased risk of chronic diseases.

The benefits of sunbeds extend beyond just vitamin D production. Historically, sunbeds were invented in the 1920s with the purpose of treating skin conditions, including skin cancer. Early studies and anecdotal evidence suggested that controlled UV exposure could have therapeutic effects. Although the prevailing discourse around sunbed use has focused on potential risks, such as skin cancer, recent peer-reviewed studies have brought new insights to the table. For example, one study investigating the relationship between sunbed use and melanoma found no increased risk for casual sunbed users. This is a crucial finding, as it challenges the common belief that all UV exposure is harmful and suggests that moderate sunbed use may not carry the same risks as excessive sun exposure.

Moreover, another study compared the melanoma risk between individuals who used sunscreen while in the sun and those who used sunbeds without sunscreen. The results were surprising: individuals who used a sunbed without sunscreen were 4.5 percent less likely to be diagnosed with melanoma than those who relied on sunscreen during sun exposure. This outcome hints at the possibility that certain chemicals and aluminium in sunscreens might contribute to skin cancer risks, more so than the controlled UV exposure from sunbeds.

These findings are further supported by research on European melanoma rates, which found intriguing results in Sweden. In Sweden, where sunbed use is strictly regulated and tanning salons are closely supervised to prevent over-exposure, there were actually fewer cases of melanoma among sunbed users than among non-users. This suggests that when sunbed use is properly managed and regulated, it can be a safe practice that might even offer protective benefits against certain types of skin cancer.

Despite these promising findings, opposition to sunbeds remains strong, primarily from cancer research organisations and pharmaceutical companies, which often emphasise the risks associated with UV exposure. It's important to consider that these organisations may have vested interests in promoting certain narratives. However, a balanced view of the current research indicates that moderate sunbed use, when conducted responsibly and within recommended guidelines, could offer several health benefits, particularly in boosting vitamin D levels and potentially reducing the risk of some diseases.

It is worth noting that vitamin D deficiency is a widespread issue, especially in regions with limited sunlight during certain times of the year. Sunbeds can be an effective solution for individuals who are unable to get sufficient sun exposure naturally. While it might seem unconventional for general practitioners to prescribe sunbed sessions for vitamin D deficiency, doing so could provide a practical and effective way to address this common health concern. As Professor Tim Oliver, a Medical Oncologist at Barts and The London Hospital, has pointed out, "Every little bit helps" when it comes to improving health outcomes.

Ultimately, while the debate over sunbed use is far from settled, the emerging research suggests that with moderate use, sunbeds could play a positive role in enhancing overall health. The key lies in responsible usage—adhering to recommended exposure times, using reputable tanning salons that ensure proper regulation, and considering individual health needs and risks. With these precautions, sunbeds could indeed offer a valuable tool for boosting vitamin D levels, supporting cardiovascular health, and potentially reducing the risk of certain cancers, contributing to a healthier lifestyle overall.

Chapter 15 - HPV Vaccine

"If over time, it turns out that the suspicion of serious adverse reactions to the vaccines is confirmed in one degree or another, it may perhaps be the biggest scandal in the history of medicine."

To explore the potential dangers of the HPV vaccine, it's crucial to delve into credible studies, scientific data, and documented facts that have raised serious concerns about its safety. In recent years, various experts and organisations have questioned the safety profile of the HPV vaccine, pointing to significant adverse reactions and the lack of comprehensive safety data.

Concerns Raised by Experts

"If over time, it turns out that the suspicion of serious adverse reactions to the vaccines is confirmed in one degree or another, it may perhaps be the biggest scandal in the history of medicine." These words, spoken by Dr. Torben Palshof, a respected Danish oncologist, highlight the potential severity of the situation. Dr. Palshof, who was involved in advising on the HPV vaccination program in Denmark, has expressed serious concerns about the safety of the vaccine. His warnings reflect a broader apprehension within the medical community regarding the HPV vaccine's potential side effects and the way regulatory agencies have managed these concerns.

Professor Peter C. Gotzsche, Director of the Nordic Cochrane Centre, and Karsten Juhl Jorgensen, Deputy Director of the same institution, have also been vocal critics of how the European Medicines Agency (EMA) has handled the safety evaluation of HPV vaccines. On May 26, 2016, they, along with other scientists, filed an official complaint with the EMA about the agency's HPV safety referral procedure. Dissatisfied with the EMA's response, they escalated their complaint to the European Ombudsman, arguing that the agency's handling of the matter was inadequate and potentially misleading. Their actions were supported by several eminent scientists who shared their concerns about the safety of the vaccine and the transparency of the regulatory process.

Evidence from Safety Reviews and Data

The EMA's handling of the HPV vaccine controversy has been criticised as a "PR disaster," particularly regarding its communication about the safety of the vaccine. The Nordic Cochrane Centre, in its complaint, pointed out that the EMA's official reports appeared to downplay or ignore concerns raised by experts regarding the vaccine's safety. For instance, while the EMA's public report suggested that there was nothing to worry about, its internal confidential report revealed that several experts had reservations about the vaccine's safety and recommended further research. This discrepancy raises significant concerns about transparency and accountability in how vaccine safety is assessed and communicated to the public.

A report from the Danish Health and Medicines Authority, intended for consideration by the EMA and rapporteurs, highlighted an alarming trend in the number of adverse reactions reported following HPV vaccination. The data from VigiBase, the World Health Organisation's global database of reported potential side effects of medicinal products, suggested an increasing number of reports involving postural orthostatic tachycardia syndrome (POTS) and related syndromes. These conditions are characterised by symptoms such as dizziness, headaches, and an abnormally fast heart rate, often accompanied by chronic fatigue-like symptoms. The report noted an over-representation of serious case reports describing a constellation of symptoms potentially consistent with a chronic fatigue-like syndrome, raising further questions about the vaccine's safety profile.

Reported Adverse Reactions

The range of suspected adverse reactions reported following HPV vaccination is extensive and troubling. Some of the most commonly reported symptoms include:

- Headaches
- Dizziness
- Nausea and vomiting
- Vision problems
- Fast heart rate
- Seizures
- Pain (including muscle and joint pain)
- Chest pain
- Numbness or tingling
- Breathing problems
- Fatigue
- Myalgic encephalomyelitis/chronic fatigue syndrome (ME/CFS)
- Postural orthostatic tachycardia syndrome (POTS)
- Gastrointestinal problems
- Autoimmune conditions
- Anxiety and conversion disorders
- Insomnia
- Paralysis

In the UK, the HPV vaccine has been associated with more reports of vaccine injuries and deaths to the Yellow Card Scheme than any other vaccine. This includes thousands of reports in categories such as gastrointestinal disorders, muscle and tissue disorders, nervous system disorders, and general disorders. The sheer volume of these reports is alarming and suggests that there may be significant safety concerns that have not been adequately addressed.

The Need for Transparency and Further Research

Given the mounting evidence and expert concerns, there is an urgent need for greater transparency and more rigorous research into the safety of the HPV vaccine. The Nordic Cochrane Centre has criticised the EMA for its lack of openness, stating, "We find the extreme level of secrecy imposed by the EMA on its working group members and other experts is inappropriate and goes against the public interest in openness and transparency about possible serious harms of the vaccine."

A study conducted by the University of Texas Medical Branch in 2015 further underscores the need for caution. This study found that vaccinated women had a higher prevalence of non-vaccine high-risk types of HPV, suggesting that the vaccine may not provide comprehensive protection against all strains of the virus and may even alter the landscape of HPV prevalence in unexpected ways.

The Importance of Doing Your Own Research

In light of these concerns, it's crucial for individuals to do their own research and make informed decisions about the HPV vaccine. While vaccines have played a vital role in public health, ensuring their safety and efficacy is paramount. Relying solely on official statements from regulatory bodies may not always provide a complete picture, especially when there are conflicting reports and evidence from credible sources suggesting potential risks.

Understanding the full scope of vaccine safety requires access to all available data, including both public and internal reports from regulatory agencies. It also requires a willingness to ask critical questions and seek out independent research and expert opinions. The decision to vaccinate is a personal one, and it should be made based on a thorough understanding of the potential benefits and risks.

Conclusion

The debate over the HPV vaccine is a reminder of the importance of transparency, accountability, and rigorous scientific inquiry in public health. As the discussion continues and more data becomes available, it is essential to keep an open mind and be prepared to reassess our understanding of vaccine safety. Only through careful consideration of all the evidence can we ensure that public health policies are truly in the best interest of the people they are meant to protect.

By staying informed and advocating for transparency, we can help ensure that vaccines remain a safe and effective tool in the fight against infectious diseases while also respecting individual autonomy and the right to make informed health decisions.

[xi] https://www.ncbi.nlm.nih.gov/pmc/articles/PMC4475239/
http://www.sciencedirect.com/science/article/pii/S0264410X16002036
https://www.ncbi.nlm.nih.gov/pmc/articles/PMC4475239/

Chapter 16 - Alzheimer's Disease

"...This study suggests that even low levels of aluminium exposure, sustained over time, may have a detrimental effect on brain health, potentially accelerating aging and increasing the risk of Alzheimer's disease."

Concluding the Studies on Aluminium and Mercury in Relation to Alzheimer's Disease

In recent years, scientific research has increasingly pointed to a potential link between exposure to certain metals, such as aluminium and mercury, and the development of Alzheimer's disease (AD). A growing body of evidence suggests that these metals could play a role in the pathogenesis of AD by contributing to neurodegenerative processes and accelerating brain aging. Here's a summary and conclusion of the findings from several key studies:

1. Aluminium and Alzheimer's Disease: A Plausible Link?

The 2011 study published in the *Journal of Alzheimer's Disease* argues that there is a significant body of experimental evidence supporting the hypothesis that chronic aluminium intoxication can reproduce neuropathological features characteristic of Alzheimer's disease. The authors suggest that the potential role of aluminium in the development of AD has been underestimated due to misconceptions about its bioavailability. The study strongly advocates for immediate measures to reduce human exposure to aluminium, positing that it may be a significant, avoidable factor contributing to the development and progression of Alzheimer's disease.

Conclusion: The study underscores the need for further investigation into aluminium's role in AD and suggests that reducing aluminium exposure could potentially mitigate some of the risks associated with the disease.

2. Increased Blood Mercury Levels in Patients with Alzheimer's Disease

This study, published in *Neural Transmission* in 1989, found elevated blood levels of mercury in patients with Alzheimer's disease. The researchers noted that these increased mercury levels were associated with higher levels of amyloid-beta (Aβ) in the cerebrospinal fluid (CSF), a hallmark of AD pathology. Interestingly, tau protein levels, another marker commonly associated with AD, were not linked to mercury levels in this study.

Conclusion: These findings suggest a potential relationship between mercury exposure and Alzheimer's disease, particularly in the context of amyloid-beta accumulation. The study indicates a need for further research into how mercury could contribute to or exacerbate the pathology of AD.

3. The Neurotoxicity of Environmental Aluminium

A 2010 study published in *Neurotoxicology* reinforces the concern about aluminium exposure, stating that aluminium should be considered a strong candidate as a subtle promoter of brain aging. The study highlights that aluminium's neurotoxic effects, although often subtle and slow to manifest, could cumulatively contribute to the aging process of the brain, thereby potentially influencing the onset and progression of Alzheimer's disease.

Conclusion: This study suggests that even low levels of aluminium exposure, sustained over time, may have a detrimental effect on brain health, potentially accelerating aging and increasing the risk of Alzheimer's disease. It calls for more attention to environmental sources of aluminium and advocates for minimising exposure.

4. Prolonged Exposure to Low Levels of Aluminium and Brain Aging

The 2014 study published in *Toxicology* discusses the epidemiological evidence indicating that aluminium exposure, even at low levels, may not be as harmless as once believed. The research suggests that prolonged exposure to aluminium could actively promote the onset and progression of Alzheimer's disease by contributing to neurodegenerative processes and accelerating brain aging.

Conclusion: This study supports the hypothesis that aluminium exposure could be a significant environmental risk factor for Alzheimer's disease. It emphasises the importance of revisiting current assumptions about aluminium's safety and the need for public health measures to limit exposure.

General Conclusion

The body of research presented here collectively suggests that there is a plausible link between exposure to metals such as aluminium and mercury and the development of Alzheimer's disease. While the exact mechanisms remain to be fully understood, the evidence points to these metals potentially playing a role in neurodegenerative processes, possibly by promoting the accumulation of toxic proteins or accelerating brain aging.

Given the serious implications of these findings, it is crucial for both the scientific community and the general public to consider the potential risks associated with metal exposure. There is a strong case for taking proactive measures to minimise exposure to these metals, particularly aluminium, which is ubiquitous in the environment and in various consumer products; vaccines, medicines, water, environmental toxins, personal hygiene products etc.

Furthermore, these studies highlight the importance of conducting thorough, independent research and being critical of widely accepted assumptions regarding environmental and health safety. As the conversation around Alzheimer's disease and potential environmental factors continues to evolve, it remains essential for individuals to stay informed and engage in ongoing research to better understand and mitigate the risks associated with these metals.

[xii] Toxicology 2014 https://www.ncbi.nlm.nih.gov/m/pubmed/24189189
https://www.ncbi.nlm.nih.gov/pmc/articles/PMC2946821
https://www.ncbi.nlm.nih.gov/m/pubmed/9588761
http://www.ncbi.nlm.nih.gov/pubmed/21157018

Chapter 17 - ADHD & Vaccines Link

"Higher rates of several neurodevelopmental disorders, including ADHD, autism, and emotional disturbances, were observed among children exposed to mercury from thimerosal-containing vaccines (TCVs)"

Conclusion: ADHD and the Impact of Vaccines on Children

Attention-Deficit/Hyperactivity Disorder (ADHD) is a neurodevelopmental condition that affects many children worldwide. Characterised by difficulties with attention, impulsiveness, and hyperactivity, ADHD can significantly impact a child's daily life, school performance, and social interactions. While the exact causes of ADHD remain complex and multifaceted, recent research has explored the potential link between certain vaccine ingredients and the development of ADHD and other neurodevelopmental disorders.

What's the Deal with Thimerosal?

Let's start by addressing the elephant in the room: thimerosal. This compound, which sounds like something straight out of a sci-fi movie, is actually an organic mercury-based preservative that has been used in various vaccines for decades. Mercury in vaccines? That might sound alarming, but thimerosal was initially added to prevent contamination and extend the shelf life of vaccines.

However, a study published in *BioMed Research International* in 2014 paints a different picture. This study reviewed over 165 studies on thimerosal and found that it might not be as harmless as once believed. Specifically, 16 studies focused on its effects on infants and children and reported a range of adverse outcomes, including developmental delays and neurodevelopmental disorders like ADHD, autism, and tics. It seems thimerosal might have more in common with a double-edged sword than a superhero.

The Mystery of Maternal Rh-Negativity and ADHD

If you're wondering what maternal Rh-negativity has to do with ADHD, you're not alone. The connection might seem a bit mysterious at first, but let's break it down. Rh-negativity refers to the absence of a specific protein on the surface of red blood cells. When a Rh-negative mother is exposed to Rh-positive blood, she might receive a shot of Rho(D) immune globulin to prevent complications during pregnancy.

According to a 2008 study published in *Neuro Endocrinology Letters*, there was a significant increase in the prevalence of maternal Rh-negativity among children with neurodevelopmental disorders, including ADHD. This study suggests that certain treatments given to Rh-negative mothers (anti-D injection) might be associated with a higher risk of neurodevelopmental disorders in their children. It's a bit like solving a detective case where all the clues point to a hidden culprit that nobody expected.

Thimerosal Exposure and Its Impact on ADHD

Now, back to our friend thimerosal. A 2008 study published in *Neurological Sciences* analysed computerised medical records and found something interesting: higher rates of several neurodevelopmental disorders, including ADHD, autism, and emotional disturbances, were observed among children exposed to mercury from thimerosal-containing vaccines (TCVs). It seems that, just like that uninvited guest who overstays their welcome, mercury exposure could linger in the body and potentially contribute to the development of these conditions.

Thimerosal-Containing Vaccines vs. Thimerosal-Free Vaccines: The Showdown

To settle the debate, another study in 2005 took a closer look at vaccines with and without thimerosal. Published in *Medical Science Monitor*, this study compared the safety of thimerosal-containing vaccines to their thimerosal-free counterparts. The results? There was a significantly increased risk of several neurodevelopmental disorders, including ADHD, autism, speech disorders, and other developmental delays, associated with thimerosal-containing vaccines. The thimerosal-free vaccines, on the other hand, had a much lower risk profile for these conditions.

This study suggests that reducing or eliminating thimerosal from vaccines could potentially lower the risk of developing neurodevelopmental disorders. It's a bit like realising that swapping out one problematic ingredient in a recipe can make a world of difference in the final dish!

Now, to make it very clear, I am NOT an advocate for any vaccines, but with such blasé facts, it does make you wonder why they wouldn't just ban thimerosal in vaccines anyway!

[xiii] https://www.ncbi.nlm.nih.gov/pubmed/24995277
https://www.ncbi.nlm.nih.gov/m/pubmed/18404135/
https://www.ncbi.nlm.nih.gov/m/pubmed/18482737/
https://www.ncbi.nlm.nih.gov/m/pubmed/15795695/

Chapter 18 - MTHFR Gene

91% of autistic children have MTHFR genetic mutation.

MTHFR Gene, Vaccines, and Autism: What's the Connection?

So, you've stumbled upon the MTHFR gene, huh? If you're like most people, you might be thinking, "Is that some newfangled text slang or a secret code?" Well, it's neither. The MTHFR gene is actually a pretty big deal in the world of genetics and health. Let's dive into what it is, how it affects us, and its surprising connections to vaccines, autism, and even the Vitamin K shot given to newborns.

The MTHFR Gene: A Brief Introduction

MTHFR stands for methylenetetrahydrofolate reductase. (Try saying that three times fast!) It's a gene that produces an enzyme responsible for breaking down the amino acid homocysteine and converting folate (a type of B vitamin) into a form the body can use. Essentially, this gene plays a key role in a process called methylation, which is crucial for detoxifying our bodies. Think of it like a microscopic cleaner, cleaning up all the mess so things don't get too toxic.

But here's the kicker: Some people have mutations in their MTHFR gene that make their bodies less efficient at this whole detox thing. This mutation can lead to a range of health issues, from increased risk of cardiovascular diseases to, you guessed it, problems with detoxifying heavy metals. And this is where things get really interesting.

The Link to Autism: What's Going On?

Recent studies have found that a whopping 91% of autistic children have an MTHFR genetic mutation. So what does this mean? Well, it turns out that if the methylation pathway is slowed down due to this mutation, the body's ability to detoxify heavy metals is also slowed down. This is a bit like having a cleaner who's overworked and understaffed—things start to pile up and get messy real quick.

Now, why does this matter when it comes to vaccines and autism? Well, vaccines and even that Vitamin K shot given at birth contain trace amounts of heavy metals and other compounds that, under normal circumstances, *could* be flushed out by the body's detox system. But if a child has the MTHFR mutation, these heavy metals might not be excreted effectively and can find a way to cross the blood-brain barrier, potentially leading to brain swelling (encephalopathy). Many parents have reported this occurring within 72 hours of vaccination, coinciding with a sudden onset of symptoms like the infamous "DTaP scream," followed by a loss of abilities such as speech and the development of autistic behaviours.

Encephalitis, Heavy Metals, and Vaccines: The Plot Thickens

So, how does all this connect to encephalitis and vaccines? Encephalitis is inflammation of the brain, which can be caused by various factors including viral infections (like the live virus in the MMR vaccine), heavy metals, or an autoimmune response. For children with the MTHFR mutation, the combination of vaccines, environmental factors, and their reduced ability to detox could contribute to the development of encephalitis.

Studies, like those conducted by Bradstreet and Geier, have shown that autistic children excrete far more heavy metals when given chelating agents compared to both vaccinated and unvaccinated controls. This suggests that autistic children, particularly those with MTHFR mutations, struggle to remove heavy metals from their bodies without assistance.

The Vitamin K Shot and Rhogam: What's the Connection?

But wait, there's more! It's not just vaccines that are under scrutiny here. The Vitamin K shot given to newborns and Rhogam injections for Rh-negative mothers may also play a role. These injections contain ingredients like aluminium or mercury (thimerosal) that are problematic for those with MTHFR mutations. If a child's detox pathways are already compromised, exposure to these substances can add to the toxic load, increasing the risk of neurodevelopmental issues.

Natural Treatments and Lifestyle Adjustments for MTHFR Mutations

Now, if you're feeling a bit overwhelmed by all this information, don't worry! The good news is there are several natural treatments and lifestyle adjustments that can help manage symptoms related to MTHFR mutations:

1. **Consume More Natural Folate, Vitamin B6, and Vitamin B12:** Skip the synthetic folic acid supplements and opt for natural folate instead. Foods like leafy greens, beans, lentils, and avocados are rich in folate and can support better methylation.

2. **Treat Digestive Problems:** Digestive health is key for those with MTHFR mutations. Avoid inflammatory foods and include gut-friendly options like probiotics, bone broth, and fermented foods.

3. **Reduce Anxiety and Depression:** Managing mental health is crucial. Incorporate omega-3 fatty acids, stress-relieving practices like meditation, and regular exercise into your routine.

4. **Protect Heart Health:** MTHFR mutations can raise homocysteine levels, increasing the risk of heart problems. Eat a heart-healthy diet, exercise, and consider supplements like magnesium and CoQ10.

5. **Discuss Medications with Your Doctor:** Some medications can worsen MTHFR mutation symptoms. Talk to your healthcare provider about any drugs you're taking.

6. **Boost Detoxification:** Support your body's detox pathways with fresh vegetable juices, activated charcoal, regular exercise, and natural detox practices like dry brushing and sauna sessions.

7. **Get Enough Quality Sleep:** Sleep is essential for overall health, especially for those with MTHFR mutations. Establish a relaxing bedtime routine and aim for seven to nine hours of sleep each night.

[xiv] https://draxe.com/mthfr-mutation/

Printed in Great Britain
by Amazon